THE *Skinny* VEGAN COOKBOOK

Zoe Hazan

HIGH CEDAR PRESS

The Skinny Vegan Cookbook
High Cedar Press
Copyright © 2020

All rights reserved. No part of this publication may be reproduced, distributed, stored in a retrieval system or transmitted in any form or by any means, including photocopying, recording, or other electronic or mechanical methods, without the prior written permission of the publisher.

The right of High Cedar Press to be identified as the authors of the work has been asserted in accordance with the Copyright, Designs and Patents Act 1988.

Published by High Cedar Press
Illustrations Copyright © 2020

THE *Skinny* VEGAN COOKBOOK

DISCLAIMER

The full contents of 'Skinny Vegan', including text, comments, graphics, images, and other content are for informational purposes only. The information is not intended to diagnose, treat, cure or prevent any illnesses or diseases. Always consult your physician before changing dietary habits.

'Skinny Vegan' does not provide specific information or advice regarding food intolerance or allergies. It is the responsibility of the reader to ensure any diagnosed or potential food intolerances are identified and excluded from the recipes.

The author and publisher make no guarantee as to the availability of ingredients mentioned in this book. Many ingredients vary in size and texture and these differences may affect the outcome of some recipes. The author has tried to make the recipes as accurate and workable as possible, however, cannot be responsible for any recipe not working.

Every effort has been made to prepare this material to ensure its accuracy, however, the author nor publisher will be held responsible if there is information deemed as inaccurate.

CONTENTS

Lasting Weight Loss	6
Veganism	8
How To Integrate Veganism Into Your Life	9
What Can You Eat?	10
Diet Swaps	11
Health and Nutrition	13
Benefits of Maintaining a Plant-Based Diet	16
Love Vegan	19

BREAKFAST

Cauliflower Hash Browns	22
Spicy Spanish Omelette	24
Tomato & Spinach Tofu Scramble	27
One-Pan Chickpea Shakshuka	29
Mini Sundried Tomato & Spinach Breakfast Quiches	31
Smokey Crisp Carrot 'Bacon'	34
Power Pancakes	36
Oatmeal Raisin Breakfast Blondies	38
Pumpkin Seed & Walnut Granola Bars	41

LUNCH

Banh Mi Buddha Bowls with Sticky Tofu	44
Moroccan Buddha Bowl with Lemon-Tahini Dressing	47
Creamy Kale & Sweet Potato Salad	50
Quinoa, Kale and Black Bean Burrito	53
Spicy Lentil & Roast Vegetable Wraps	56
Stuffed Sweet Potato with Quinoa Tabbouleh	58
Creamy Broccoli & Red Lentil Detox Soup	61

MAINS

Vegetable Stir-Fry with Ginger Miso Sauce	65
Caribbean Jerk Tofu with Coconut Quinoa	67
Chana Masala with Spinach & Peas	69
Mexican Style Stuffed Peppers	71
Sicilian Eggplant Rolls with Tofu Ricotta	73
Ratatouille Pasta Bake	76

THE *Skinny* VEGAN COOKBOOK

15 Minute Creamy Avocado-Basil Pasta	79
Crispy Mediterranean Tortilla Pizza	81
The Ultimate Quinoa Crust Pizza	83
Red Lentil Dhal with Carrot & Sweet Potato	85
Mujadara (Lentils & Rice with Caramelised Onions	87
Cauliflower Dhansak	89
Mushroom & Chickpea Pitta Burger	92
15 Minute Garlic & Mushroom Quinoa	94

SIDES

Spinach, Lemon & Chickpea Brown Rice Pilaf	97
Patatas Bravas with a Creamy Garlic Drizzle	99
Tikka (Indian Spiced Cauliflower Rice	102
Crispy Baked Zucchini Tater Tots	104
Fat-Free Crispy Potatoes	106
Carrot & Parsnip Fries	108
Spicy Maple-Garlic Roasted Cauliflower	110
Butter Bean Dip with Garlic & Herbs	112

DESSERTS & TREATS

Silky Smooth Chocolate Pudding	115
Chocolate Quinoa Crunch Bars	117
4 Ingredient Healthy Fudgy Brownies	119
Baked Red Velvet Doughnuts	121
Chocolate Orange Chia Pudding	124
Carrot Cake Bites with 'Cream Cheese' Frosting	126
150-Calorie Chocolate Coconut Cupcakes	129
Chocolate & Almond Energy Bites	131
Super Seed Omega Boost Energy Bars	133

EXTRAS

Chocolate Hazelnut Milk (Nutella Milk)	136
Easy Homemade Tortillas	138
Roasted Chickpeas 3 Ways	140
Cumin & Cayenne Super Seed Crackers Healthy	143
Oil Free Hummus	145
10-Minute Fat-Free Gravy	147
Healthy Oil-Free Mayonnaise	149
Sour Cream & Chive Popcorn	151

LASTING WEIGHT LOSS...

WITHOUT GIVING UP WHAT YOU LOVE!

It is no secret that most of us want to lose a bit of weight. It is probably one of the most common problems we face on a day-to-day basis. In fact so much so that Americans spends over $35 billion each year on weight loss products.

Despite this the obesity rate remains higher than ever. This is because pill and supplements cannot replace a balanced and healthy diet.

When someone says 'diet' though it usually means depriving yourself or following some crazy regime in which 5 days of the week you have to starve yourself, or where you can only eat red meat on weekdays.

These are neither healthy nor sustainable ways of living and what happens with these 'diets' is that you will hit your target weight and then go back to your old eating habits. With this book and plant based eating you do not need to restrict yourself and you won't be constantly craving food as you will be filling yourself with plant-based goodness.

Meat, dairy, eggs, cheese, etc are all packed with calories and fat when compared to their plant counterparts. This means you can eat a lot more food when eating plant-based, but don't worry it's not just lettuce leaves...

THE *Skinny* VEGAN COOKBOOK

As you will see from this book this doesn't just mean eating salads all the time. This book is packed with exciting recipes that utilise ingredients such as tofu, quinoa and cauliflower in unbelievably delicious ways. You will get the same rich and satisfying dishes but with half the calories of the non-vegan alternative. You will be able to eat breakfast, lunch, dinner as well as a dessert now and then, all whilst losing weight!

A few other factors for losing weight are getting enough sleep, drinking enough water and doing 20 minutes of brisk walking a day (at least). All these help your body to operate efficiently and help your metabolism.

One more tip we would give is that it is ok to have a dessert, but if you do, have it as early as possible! Our bodies are awful at processing and metabolising food the later it gets, so in actual terms, every calorie eaten in the evening counts for up to double than the morning. So 100 calories in the morning, is equivalent to 150 calories past 8pm and the later you eat, the heavier each calorie becomes!

All that being said the main thing is to have fun discovering new meals that you probably didn't think you could have on a diet...

Good Luck!

VEGANISM

The vegetarian revolution is a culinary movement has truly gathered steam over the past few years.

According to a recent report, 1 in 8 UK adults now follows either a vegetarian or vegan diet and this number reaches 1 in 4 for those between the ages of 16-25.

Whether you are seeking a way to optimize your own health and well-being, or if you are concerned about reducing animal suffering and the environment - being part of the vegan movement is definitely a great path to follow.

Veganism is a stricter form of vegetarianism. For many vegetarians, it's also the next step. Whether a vegan omnivore or vegan, the "Skinny Vegan" series is here to help you with quick and easy recipes to prepare.

We have done the trialling and perfecting for you and have put together this Skinny Vegan Cookbook which proves you can eat well whilst on a diet. All these recipes have been tested and created from years of experimentation.

There are countless stories of how effective veganism can be for weight loss and if you follow this book, it will be for you too!

HOW TO INTEGRATE VEGANISM INTO YOUR LIFE

Vegans only eat foods that come from plant-based sources. Western cultures rely heavily on meat and fish, so it is perfectly fine to transition slowly as you may need time to adjust to this new way of living. The transition from being a meat-eater to a vegan needs to be slow and well planned in order for it to be successful.

First and foremost, you need to make sure that you understand the basic nutritional facts about vegan ingredients. Proportions and size of servings are important for you to thrive on a vegan diet and you will need to plan your meals and snacks carefully.

You can bring health and compassion to your table without being a full-time vegan. Many cultures have adopted a part-time vegan lifestyle.

In India, where animal-based products are consumed far less than in the Western world, it's not uncommon to have a certain number of days in a week or even months in a year when a vegan diet rules.

Veganism doesn't mean that you have to eat leaves and lettuce all day or miss out on your favorite foods. It is very important to learn the nutritional value of ingredients and to plan varied meals throughout the day. Your body will let you know quickly enough if it doesn't get the necessary nutrients.

WHAT CAN YOU EAT?

If it has a face, eyes, fins, feet or wings, ban it from your plate! If it's sourced from a plant, go for it. It gets a little more involved and less straightforward with by-products. For example, can you eat honey? The answer is no, as it's an animal by-product.

If your main interest in adopting a plant-based diet is the effect it will have on your weight loss, then you don't need to worry about this. If you are following a vegan diet but having a bit of meat, or fish here and there that's fine.

As the plan is to lose weight, we would aruge for cutting out cheese completely. Apart from the fact that it contains the highly addictive chemical Casomorphin (an opoid used to ensure a calf nurses from its mother), it is also high in saturated fats, salt and calories.

We would also suggest permanently switching to a plant based milk if you haven't already. Countless studies have shown the negative effects cow's milk has on our bodies. Given the number of delicious plant-based alternatives, it should be a simple switch.

DIET SWAPS

Replacing animal products for plant-based produce will open up a world of wonderful possibilities.

Milk and Dairy Products

Not all milks are from animals - such as soy, rice, oat and almond. They are all low in fat and make a wonderful alternative, providing you with the same creamy texture that you would find in dairy milk. There is a vast array of vegan alternatives to dairy-based products for you to explore.

Meat or Sausages Replacement

Fermented soybeans known as tempeh is full of protein and is easily available. Tofu is also very common and can be pressed to be rid of excess moisture then marinated to retain flavor. You will find that due to the growth of veganism your supermarkets will have numerous meat replacements, usually in the freezer aisle, that taste excellent and mimic the texture of meat very closely. They are also usually lower calorie than their meaty counterparts.

Eggs

Eggs are one of the most difficult ingredients to substitute. The key is to think about the function they performed in the recipes. If you are looking for a binding agent - cornstarch, arrowroot, tahini, bread crumbs, and mashed potatoes are good replacements. If you need a raising agent baking powder usually works well. There are many alternative products on the market including a powder which makes delicious scrambled 'eggs', as well as various egg replacers that are suitable for baking.

So go ahead and veganaise your dishes - you won't even notice the difference!

HEALTH AND NUTRITION

*T*he food you eat can be either the safest and most powerful form of medicine or the slowest form of poison -

Ann Wigmore

Not only does the vegan diet provide numerous health benefits including a reduced risk of contracting heart disease, obesity, hypertension, and diabetes, it also provides social, moral and environmental benefits.

When adopting a vegan lifestyle it is important to know a few basic facts about nutrition and to be careful when planning meals by making sure that your diet contains not only plenty of vegetables and fresh fruits, but also whole grains, beans, legumes, nuts, and seeds. A vegan diet should be packed with B, C, and E, folates, magnesium, and iron.

Let take a look at the various vegan sources for these different vitamins and minerals so that you can perfectly balance your vegan diet:

Vitamin B

A vegan diet is packed with vitamin B which is found in fresh fruits and vegetables. There are several kinds of sources for vitamin B but the most reliable sources include:
- Pulses
- Beans
- Whole grains
- Potatoes

- Banana
- Nutritional yeast
- Chili peppers

Vitamin B12

Sourcing vitamin B12 poses difficulties for vegans as it is commonly found in animal products, so in order to eliminate any problems, your diet might have to be complemented with either fortified food or supplements. Milks and cereals are often fortified.

Vitamin C

Essential for strong bones and teeth, vitamin C is found in food items such as:

- Tomato and tomato sauces
- Dark leafy greens
- Fresh juices
- Cereals
- Berries

Vitamin E

Like all other vitamins, Vitamin E plays many roles, among others it has an important neurological function and is responsible for repairing tissues and wounds.

The best sources of Vitamin E for vegans are:

- Oils (Olive, Coconut, Nut oils)
- Avocados
- Kiwis
- Tomatoes

- Pumpkins
- Mangos
- Papayas

Iron

Many vegetables contain iron. It is very important to include iron in your diet as it is essential for blood production. Plant-based iron (non-heme iron) should be consumed with Vitamin C for maximum absorption. Iron is synonymous with Popeye's fondness for spinach but did you know that the following are packed with Iron too:

- Potatoes
- Lentils
- Almond
- Flax and pumpkin seeds
- Chickpeas

BENEFITS OF MAINTAINING A PLANT-BASED DIET

In addition to financial benefits (eating a vegan diet generally costs less, because meat can be expensive, whereas cans of chickpeas or beans are extremely inexpensive), there are a wide range of well-documented health and nutritional benefits to going vegan. We have talked about the overarching benefits, such as weight loss and an increase in energy levels. Now let's focus on some of the smaller positive outcomes of a vegan diet.

Health benefits:

1. *Better breath:* Due to the levels of acids needed to digest meats and animal products, halitosis reduction can be a significant beneficial effect of going vegan. Who doesn't want to be able to hit the gym without morning breath?

2. *Reduced body odour:* As with bad breath, body odour tends to be reduced in those that do not eat meat. This further reduces your dependence on harsh chemicals found in many antiperspirants and deodorants, and makes working out an overall more pleasant experience.

3. *Lessening of allergy symptoms:* For those who struggle to alleviate allergy symptoms without resorting to over-the-counter medicines like antihistamines, a vegan diet may be the answer. Reducing meat, dairy, and egg consumption has

been linked to a reduction in allergy symptoms as well as skin conditions.

4. *Stronger hair and nails:* Both hair and nails become stronger and healthier during periods of veganism, meaning you will not only feel better, but look better too.

Nutritional benefits:

1. *Eggs:* By avoiding eggs, and replacing these with vegan substitutes like chia seeds or ready-made vegan egg mixes, you will help to keep your cholesterol levels at bay. Eating too many eggs can raise cholesterol, as can red meat and too much saturated fat. Low cholesterol is imperative for successful weight loss and long term body health.

2. *Mercury:* Fish and shellfish can both contain low levels of mercury, a known toxin that never leaves our body once it's ingested. Therefore, pregnant women and young children are advised not to each too much fish. Ingesting mercury can even lead to serious brain conditions in some rare, but severe, cases.

3. *Sugar:* Everyone knows that eating too much sugar is bad for your health. Some vegans tend to avoid processed sugar entirely, because activated charcoal made from animal bones is used in the sugar refinement process. As vegans also shun using animals as a commodity, this would be a valid

reason not to eat it – not to mention the benefits of low fat levels in successful weight loss!

4. *Fibre and antioxidants:* Eating vegan will automatically increase your fibre intake, as more of your plate is filled with fruit, vegetables, and whole grains. Fibre is known to be key in reducing cholesterol and helping to prevent colorectal cancer, and is crucial to digestion as well. Antioxidants are also linked to cancer prevention, as well as repairing cell damage that could occur while exercising.

5. *Carbohydrates:* Often the first to be sacrificed on a diet. The solution to losing weight is not to cut out all carbohydrates. In fact studies have shown that the group with the highest BMI are meat-eaters, then vegetarians, and the lowest BMI are vegans. What is important is to cut out refined carbohydrates and only fill your body with whole-foods. So for example switching out white rice for brown rice and doing the same with other processed and refined carbohydrates. Whole and natural carbohdrates actually aid in your body processes and metabolism and ultimately in weight loss.

LOVE VEGAN

Quick and Easy to Prepare

Nobody wants to spend hours in the kitchen to make dinner following a long, hard day. This is a good reason to adopt plant-based cooking as a staple in your household. A lot of the dishes are fast and easy to prepare. And despite some having a relatively long ingredient list, most just need to simmer for a while which doesn't require your presence.

Great for the Waist

Aside from speed in preparation, there are also lots of other advantages. Traditionally vegetable-based, it's an excellent diet for slimmers and it will provide you with limitless vitality whilst leaving you full and satiated.

Straightforward, Natural Ingredients

Our recipes have been specially crafted to ensure you will not need to waste time searching for the ingredients within our recipes as they are straightforward and everything you need can be found in farmers' markets or your local supermarket.

Many of the recipes call for spices that are used to enhance the flavors of raw vegetables but also to protect against food-borne infection. If at first, you need to invest in jars of spices don't worry, you will be able to use the spices again and again.

The aim of this book and the Love Vegan series is to make eating and cooking food, which is good for your body, a pleasure and to cut down on the fuss of preparation.

Tried and Tested Recipes

All the recipes in this book have been carefully tried and tested. We have taken all the weeknight staple classics and have slightly adapted them to remove animal products.

The best thing about cooking vegan foods is that most variations of dishes will only take a fraction of the time that cooking the meat or fish versions would have taken.

We hope you enjoy this cookbook and gain back precious time to do what you love by reducing the amount of time it takes to prepare and cook dinner each night!

BREAKFAST

CAULIFLOWER HASH BROWNS

These cauliflower hash browns have all the flavour and crispy goodness of traditional hash browns but without the guilt! Fried in only a tablespoon of oil, they are a great way to reduce your carb intake and lower your daily calories whilst being surprisingly delicious.

Preparation Time
5 minutes

Total Time
15 minutes

Makes
6 patties

Per Patty: Calories: 74 | Fat: 2.6g | Saturated Fat: 0.2g

INGREDIENTS

- ½ large head of cauliflower, broken into florets
- 3 scallions, finely chopped
- ¼ cup chickpea flour
- 1 tbsp cornstarch or arrowroot starch
- ½ large head of cauliflower, broken into florets
- 3 scallions, finely chopped
- ¼ cup chickpea flour
- 1 tbsp cornstarch or arrowroot starch
- 2 tbsp nutritional yeast, optional
- ½ tsp salt
- ½ tsp black pepper
- 2 tbsp dairy free milk
- 1 tbsp olive oil or low-cal spray oil

DIRECTIONS

Place the cauliflower in a food processor and process until it resembles small grains of rice. If you do not have a food processor you can use a box grater. Transfer to a large bowl.

Add the scallions, chickpea flour, cornstarch, nutritional yeast, salt, pepper, and milk. Mix thoroughly adding another tablespoon of milk if the mixture is too dry and not holding together.

Heat olive oil in a skillet over medium-high heat. Move the skillet around, spreading the olive oil to cover the surface.

Divide the batter into 6 and mould them into oval shaped hash browns. Fry 2-3 patties at a time, making sure to not overcrowd the pan. Reduce the heat to medium and fry each patty for 4-5 minutes, then flip over and fry for another 4-5 minutes.

Repeat with the remaining batter and serve immediately while golden brown and crispy.

SPICY SPANISH OMELETTE

Traditionally known as tortilla de patatas, this ingenious recipe uses chickpea flour as a replacement for eggs, creating a soft and fluffy 'egg' base. The omelette can be served hot or cold, and also makes a filling lunch due to the addition of potatoes. The secret ingredient is black salt, which will provide a slightly 'eggy' flavour, but it is not essential if you can't find it.

Preparation Time
10 minutes

Total Time
40 minutes

Makes
8 slices

Per Slice: Calories: 132 | Fat: 2.8g | Saturated Fat: 0.4g

INGREDIENTS

- 1 tbsp olive oil, divided
- 1 large clove garlic
- 1 medium red onion, sliced
- 3 medium waxy potatoes, cut into ¼ inch round slices
- 1 cup / 120g chickpea flour
- 240ml / 1 cup water
- ⅛ tsp black salt (kala namak), optional
- ½ tsp smoked paprika
- ¼-½ tsp cayenne pepper
- ½ tsp sea salt (use ¼ tsp sea salt if using black salt)
- ½ tsp black pepper

DIRECTIONS

Heat ½ a tablespoon of oil in a large skillet. Arrange the potato slices so that they form a single layer over the surface of the skillet - you may need to do this in batches as you don't want the potatoes to overlap. Fry on each side for around 4-5 minutes until soft and starting to brown on the edges. Transfer to a paper towel lined plate and continue with remaining potato slices.

Once all the potatoes have cooked remove them from the skillet and set aside on a plate. Fry the onion for 2-3 minutes (you do not need to wash the pan after removing the potatoes) until they soften then add the garlic, frying for a minute.

Place the chickpea flour, water, black salt, paprika, cayenne and seasoning in a food processor and process until you have a smooth batter. Transfer to a large bowl.

Once the potatoes and onions are cooked add them to the bowl and gently mix to combine.

Heat the skillet up once more with the remaining half tablespoon of olive oil. Once the oil is hot pour in the batter and gently tilt the pan for it to evenly spread over the surface.

Fry for 7-8 minutes or until the bottom has become firm then gently flip it over and fry for 6-7 minutes on the other side. The best way to flip the omelette without it breaking is to slide it onto a plate and then transfer it back to the skillet.

Remove from the heat, cut into 8 slices and serve hot or cold with a salad. The omelette will keep for 3 days in an airtight container in the fridge.

TOMATO & SPINACH TOFU SCRAMBLE

This breakfast is an incredile cholesterol-free replacement for scrambled eggs. If you are able to source black salt it will add an authentic 'eggy' flavor to the tofu scramble (without being too overpowering!). The texture is very similar to eggs and this dish is flavoured wonderfully with cumin, paprika and turmeric. The tofu is an incredible source of protein and gives you the complete range of aminos you need.

Preparation Time
10 minutes

Total Time
20 minutes

Makes
2 servings

Per Serving: Calories: 392 | Fat: 15.7g | Saturated Fat: 2.9g

INGREDIENTS

- 1 tbsp olive oil
- 12.5oz / 350g firm tofu
- ½ red onion, thinly sliced
- 1 large garlic clove, finely chopped
- 1 large ripe tomato, seeds removed and chopped
- ½ tsp red chili flakes (or less depending on heat preference)
- ½ tsp ground turmeric
- ¼ tsp paprika
- ½ tsp cumin
- ½ tsp Kala namak / black salt (or substitute regular salt)
- ½ tsp black pepper
- 1 packed cup spinach, washed
- 2-4 slices of thick sourdough bread, toasted
- ½ avocado (optional)

DIRECTIONS

To start, remove tofu from packaging and press between two towels to remove excess water. You can use something weighted, such as a large saucepan or a heavy chopping board and place this on top of the tofu to squeeze out as much moisture as possible for a minimum of 10 minutes. This process will allow the tofu to absorb much more flavour.

While the tofu is being pressed, heat olive oil in a large pan. Once the oil is hot add the red onion and saute for 3-4 minutes until soft then add the garlic, tomato, red chili flakes, turmeric, cumin, paprika, salt and pepper.

Add the tofu to a bowl and break it up using a fork or your hands so that it resembles scrambled eggs then add it to the pan, increasing the heat to medium. Cook for 5 minutes, stirring frequently, then add the spinach and cook for 3 minutes until the spinach has wilted.

Serve immediately on toasted bread and with avocado if you wish.

ONE-PAN CHICKPEA SHAKSHUKA

Shakshuka is a popular Middle-Eastern dish made up of an aromatically spiced tomato sauce with poached eggs. This vegan version substitutes eggs with protein packed and cholesterol free chickpeas, but still retains the exotic Middle Eastern flavours. This makes a fantastic weekend breakfast served with crusty bread, but can also be enjoyed for lunch or dinner.

Preparation Time
10 minutes

Total Time
35 minutes

Makes
4 servings

Per Serving: Calories: 453 | Fat: 9.2g | Saturated Fat: 1.4g

INGREDIENTS

½ tbsp olive oil
1 medium white onion, chopped
4 large cloves garlic, finely chopped
1 red chili, finely chopped
2 tsp ground cumin
½ tbsp smoked paprika
1 tsp ground coriander
½ tsp cayenne pepper

½ tsp sea salt
¼ tsp ground black pepper
1 ½ cups / 225g canned or cooked chickpeas
½ cup kalamata olives, sliced
2 tbsp sundried tomatoes (the variety soaked in oil), roughly chopped

1 heaped tbsp tomato pure
½ cup / 120ml vegetable stock
½ tsp brown sugar or coconut sugar
1 can (15oz / 420g) chopped tomatoes
4 tbsp fresh parsley, chopped
4 tbsp fresh cilantro, chopped
Warm bread or medium pita (65g pita), to serve

DIRECTIONS

Heat oil in a large skillet and once hot saute the onions for 3-4 minutes. Add the garlic, chili and all of the spices and cook for a minute, stirring constantly.

Add the tomato puree and brown sugar, stirring for 10 seconds then pour in the chopped tomatoes and vegetable stock. Bring everything to a boil then reduce to a simmer for 10 minutes, stirring frequently, until the sauce has thickened.

Add the chickpeas, olives and sundried tomatoes and simmer for another 10 minutes until the sauce has thickened even more.

Remove from the heat, stir in the parsley and cilantro and serve with warm bread or toasted pita.

MINI SUNDRIED TOMATO & SPINACH BREAKFAST QUICHES

These make-ahead mini-quiches are perfect for when you're on the go or don't have time to make breakfast. For anyone that isn't a breakfast person, these little delights are a great snack. They're savoury and quichey (for want of a better word!). Aside from each quiche containing just 57 calories per quiche, they are also extremely cheap to make and great if you want to use up any veggies in the fridge.

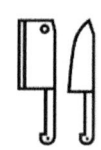

Preparation Time
10 minutes

Total Time
25 minutes

Makes
12 mini quiches

Per Quiche: Calories: 57 | Fat: 1.1g | Saturated Fat: 0.1g

INGREDIENTS

Low-calorie cooking spray
½ small red onion, finely chopped
2 garlic cloves, minced
Large handful spinach leaves, washed
1 cup / 125g chickpea flour, sieved
1 ½ cup water
4 tbsp nutritional yeast
¼ tsp baking powder
A pinch of black salt (optional)
½ tsp kosher salt
½ tsp black pepper
8 sun dried tomatoes*, finely chopped

If you are using the dried variety soak them in lukewarm water for 15-20 minutes before adding to the batter. If you are using the kind that sits in oil, drain well and pat off as much oil as possible using a paper towel.

DIRECTIONS

Preheat the oven to 400°F / 200°C . Prepare a muffin tin by spraying a little cooking oil into each mould.

Heat a skillet with a spritz of cooking oil and saute the onions for 5 minutes until they have softened. Add the garlic and spinach and stir continuously to prevent the garlic from burning until the spinach has wilted. Remove from the heat and set aside to cool down a little.

In a large bowl whisk together the chickpea flour, water, nutritional yeast, baking powder, salt, and pepper until completely smooth and no lumps remain.

Add the onion mixture along with the sundried tomatoes and transfer to a large jug which will make it easier to pour the batter into the muffin moulds. Alternatively, you could use a ladle.

Evenly pour the mixture into the muffin tins and bake for 15-20 minutes or until the quiches have firmed up and the top has browned a little.

Use a sharp knife to circle the edge of the muffin moulds while the quiches are still hot to remove them easily.

Cool on a wire rack for 5-10 minutes to firm up before serving.

SMOKY CRISP CARROT 'BACON'

This smoky, curly and super crispy carrot bacon is delicious served in a tofu scramble, a sandwich, as a salad topping or as a side for just about anything! It is surprisingly easy to make - just be alert during the last 10 minutes in the oven as it is prone to burning. Whilst you can tell the difference between this and bacon... at a fraction of the calories it is the perfect substitute.

Preparation Time
5 minutes

Total Time
25 minutes

Makes
2 servings

Per Serving: Calories: 117 | Fat: 7g | Saturated Fat: 0.9g

INGREDIENTS

- 1 large carrot, peeled
- 1 tbsp oil (olive, rapeseed, canola etc)
- 1 tsp paprika
- 1/8 tsp cayenne pepper
- 1 tbsp maple syrup, agave nectar or brown rice syrup
- 1 tsp tamari sauce
- 1 tsp liquid smoke (optional)

DIRECTIONS

Preheat the oven to 400°F / 200°C. Line a baking tray with parchment paper.

THE Skinny VEGAN COOKBOOK

Chop the top and bottom of the carrot off and slice it very thin, lengthways, using a sharp knife or a mandoline slicer.

Mix the oil, paprika, cayenne, syrup, tamari and liquid smoke together in a medium bowl then add the carrots and mix well until the carrot slices are well coated.

Transfer the carrot bacon onto the baking tray in a single layer, making sure they do not overlap.

Bake for 20-25 minutes until they start to curl and brown slightly at the edges. Check frequently after 20 minutes to ensure they do not burn.

FLUFFY AMERICAN PANCAKES

Blast your body with these energy packed fluffy pancakes. They are super versatile and can be served with anything from maple syrup to pecans and are perfect for the weekend. Just because you're trying to lose weight, doesn't mean you can't have fun.

Preparation Time
5 minutes

Total Time
10 minutes

Makes
2 large pancakes

Per Pancake: Calories: 363 | Fat: 5.3g | Saturated Fat: 0.9g

INGREDIENTS

- 1 cup rolled oats
- 1 large ripe banana
- 1 cup dairy-free milk (almond, coconut or soy)
- 1-2 tbsp maple syrup or agave nectar
- ½ tsp baking powder
- ¼ tsp baking soda
- Pinch of salt
- 1 tsp vanilla extract
- Oil or vegan butter for frying
- Extra syrup, to serve
- Fresh or frozen berries, to serve

DIRECTIONS

Place all ingredients (except oil for frying, syrup and berries for serving) in a food processor or high-speed blender and pulse until you have a smooth batter.

Heat a teaspoon of oil or vegan butter in a skillet over medium heat. Once hot use a ladle to scoop a large spoonful into the center of the frying pan. Allow it to cook on one side, without flipping, until bubbles appear on the surface and the edges start to brown, around 2-4 minutes. Flip and cook on the other side for 1-2 minutes. Repeat with the remaining batter.

Serve with a drizzle of syrup and fresh berries.

OATMEAL RAISIN BREAKFAST BLONDIES

These oatmeal raisin blondies have a soft chewy center and amazingly crisp edges - exactly how a blondie should be. Whilst these aren't classified as super-low calorie, given how delicious and decadent they are, they are really reasonable at only 200 calories a bar. They're also packed full of good energy in the form of oats and nut butter. So if you have to indulge, it is better to do it with something unrefined and nutritious!

Preparation Time
10 minutes

Total Time
20 minutes

Makes
8 bars

Per Bar: Calories: 203 | Fat: 9.3g | Saturated Fat: 0.8g

INGREDIENTS

For the Blondies:
- ½ cup coconut sugar
- ½ cup natural nut butter (almond, peanut or cashew)
- 1 tsp vanilla extract
- ½ cup + 2 tbsp almond or oat flour*
- ¼ cup rolled oats
- ¾ tsp baking powder
- ½ tsp ground cinnamon
- ¼ tsp ground nutmeg
- ¼ tsp sea salt
- 3 tbsp unsweetened dairy free milk
- ¼ cup raisins

THE Skinny VEGAN COOKBOOK

DIRECTIONS

You can make your own oat or almond flour by pulsing oats in a food processor for a few minutes until it turns into a fine powder.

Preheat the oven to 350°F / 175°C. Line an 8x8" brownie tin with parchment paper.

In a large bowl mix together the sugar, nut butter and vanilla using an electric whisk or stand mixer until fully combined, around 1 minute.

In a separate bowl combine the oat flour, oats, baking powder, cinnamon, nutmeg, and salt.

Add the oat flour along with the dairy free milk to the nut butter mixture and beat on low for 15 seconds, increasing to medium for another 15 seconds. The dough should have pulled together, however, if it appears to dry add ½ tbsp more milk. If it seems too wet add ½ tbsp more oat flour.

Add the raisins and beat for 10-15 seconds until they are evenly incorporated.

Transfer to the lined brownie tin and smooth the top over with the back of a spoon.

Bake for 25-30 minutes or until the top has cracked, the edges are brown, and a toothpick comes out clean.

Allow the blondies to cool down for 10-15 minutes then slice into 8 bars.

PUMPKIN SEED & WALNUT GRANOLA BARS

Whip up these crunchy, oaty and nutty bars for a healthy breakfast or snack on the go. You can play around with the ingredients and sub walnuts for any other nut of choice or even add dried fruit. They provide great long-lasting energy and are surprisingly filling!

Preparation Time
15 minutes

Total Time
35 minutes

Makes
9 granola bars

Per Serving: Calories: 271 | Fat: 11.9g | Saturated Fat: 3.7g

INGREDIENTS

2 cups old fashioned oats
⅓ cup pumpkin seeds
½ cup unsweetened applesauce
1 ½ tsp vanilla extract
¼ cup maple syrup
2 tbsp coconut oil
1 tsp cinnamon
3 tbsps raisins or sultanas
½ cup walnuts, roughly chopped
¼ tsp salt

DIRECTIONS

Preheat the oven to 350°F / 175°C and line a 9x9" brownie tin with parchment paper.

Pour the oats and pumpkin seeds onto a separate baking tray and toast in the oven for 8-10 minutes until lightly browned.

Keep an eye on the oven as the oats and seeds can burn quickly.

In a small saucepan combine applesauce, vanilla, maply syrup, coconut oil and cinnamon until melted then remove from the heat.

Once the oats and seeds have finished toasting add the raisins, walnuts and salt and mix well. Pour the wet mixture into the dry mixture and stir until combined, adding a tablespoon more applesauce if the mixture is too dry.

Transfer to the brownie tin and smooth the top with the back of a spoon or spatula.

Allow to set in the fridge for 2-3 hours before slicing and serving.

Store in an airtight container for up to a week.

LUNCH

BANH MI BUDDHA BOWLS WITH STICKY TOFU

The beauty of Buddha bowls lies in their versatility as you can play around with the ingredients by using whatever you have in the fridge or freezer. They make a hearty and colourful lunch or a healthy and low-calorie dinner and are super easy to throw together. This version has a delicious Asian sticky glaze for the tofu.

Preparation Time
10 minutes

Total Time
20 minutes

Makes
2 servings

Per Serving: Calories: 654 | Fat: 39.2g | Saturated Fat: 7g

INGREDIENTS

For the Buddha Bowls:
6oz / 170g rice noodles
1 medium carrot, peeled and grated
½ cup cucumber, thinly sliced
¾ cup red cabbage, grated
½ cup edamame
1 avocado, sliced

For the Sticky tofu:
14oz / 340g extra firm tofu
1 tbsp sesame oil (you can also use olive, canola or another high heating oil)
1 tbsp soy sauce
2 tbsp hoisin sauce
1 tsp sriracha
1 tbsp water

2 tbsp sesame seeds
1 handful fresh cilantro, chopped
2-3 scallions, chopped

DIRECTIONS

To start, remove tofu from packaging and press between two towels to remove excess water. You can use something weighted, such as a large saucepan or a heavy chopping board and place this on top of the tofu to squeeze out as much moisture as possible for a minimum of 10 minutes. This process will allow the tofu to absorb much more flavour. After 10 minutes chop the tofu into cubes.

While the tofu is being pressed prepare all Buddha bowl ingredients. Cook the rice noodles according to packet directions and chop all of the vegetables. Divide the noodles into two bowls then top with equal amounts of all other ingredients, except the sesame seeds, scallions, and cilantro. Set aside.

In a small bowl combine soy sauce, hoisin, sriracha, and water. Set aside.

Heat a large skillet with sesame oil. Once hot add the tofu cubes and fry for 2 minutes without flipping, then turn each cube over and fry again for another 2 minutes. Continue until all sides have browned and are crispy.

Add the sticky sauce to the pan and stir quickly to coat all cubes. Remove from the heat and spoon onto the Buddha bowls then top with sesame seeds, scallions, and cilantro.

MOROCCAN BUDDHA BOWL WITH LEMON-TAHINI DRESSING

This hearty bowl of goodness is filled with aromatic Moroccan flavors. The colours alone make it incredibly appetizing, plus you will feel energized and healthy for hours after. Although it seems like there are a lot of ingredients the process is actually very simple. A lot of the ingredients are made up of spices so don't be put off by the length of the ingredients list!

Preparation Time
10 minutes

Total Time
30 minutes

Makes
2 servings

Per Serving: Calories: 687 | Fat: 32.5g | Saturated Fat: 5.6g

INGREDIENTS

For the Buddha Bowl:

1 medium sweet potato, cut into equal sized chunks
1 red onion, cut into thick slices
¼ tsp salt
¼ tsp black pepper
1 tsp ground cumin
½ tsp ground coriander
¼ tsp ground cinnamon
1 tbsp olive oil, divided
1 tbsp maple syrup
1 tsp each: garlic powder / paprika / cumin
¼ tsp salt
¼ tsp pepper
1 cup couscous, cooked
1 cup chopped red cabbage

¼ tsp chili powder
1 can (15oz / 420g) chickpeas, drained and rinsed
1 cup baby spinach, chopped
1 avocado, sliced

For the Lemon Tahini Dressing:
2 tbsp tahini
3 tbsp lemon juice
1 small clove garlic, finely chopped
2 tbsp warm water
2 tsp maple syrup
¼ tsp cayenne pepper
¼ tsp turmeric
Salt to taste

DIRECTIONS

Preheat the oven to 350°F / 175°C. Line a baking tray with parchment paper.

Place the sweet potato cubes and red onion in a mixing bowl and drizzle over ½ tablespoon of olive oil, coating all cubes. Add the salt, pepper, cumin, coriander, cinnamon, and chili powder, and mix well to coat.

Transfer to the baking tray and roast for 15-20 minutes (depending on the size of the potato chunks). Check to see whether the potato is cooked by piercing a cube with a fork.

Whilst the sweet potato is cooking, prepare the chickpeas by adding them to a large mixing bowl along with the maple syrup, garlic, paprika, cumin, salt, and pepper.

Heat oil in a skillet over medium heat then add the chickpeas for 5-7 minutes, stirring frequently, to prevent the spices from burning, until they are heated throughout. If the mixture seems too dry add a tablespoon of water at a time. Remove from the heat and set aside.

Divide the couscous between two bowls, using the grains as a base for the buddha bowl. Add the red cabbage, spinach, avocado, cooked chickpeas, roasted sweet potato, and red onion.

For the Lemon-Tahini Dressing:

Whisk all ingredients together in a bowl until fully combined.

Drizzle Lemon-Tahini Dressing on top once the Buddha Bowl is ready.

CREAMY KALE & SWEET POTATO SALAD

We all know how nutritionally dense kale is but that doesn't take away from the fact that it isn't the most exciting vegetable. This salad is a great way to include this nutrient powerhouse in your diet - and actually enjoy it! Kale is combined with sweet potato, chickpea and lots of wonderfully aromatic spices, then drizzled with a creamy tahini-maple dressing. You'll be reaching for seconds before you know it!

Preparation Time
10 minutes

Total Time
30 minutes

Makes
4 servings

Per Serving: Calories: 292 | Fat: 19g | Saturated Fat: 2.7g

INGREDIENTS

For the Salad:

- 1 bunch of kale, washed + ribs and stem discarded
- 2 cups sweet potatoes, diced
- 1 red pepper, seeds removed and diced
- 1 (15oz / 420g) can chickpeas, drained and rinsed
- ½ tsp each: ground cumin, coriander & turmeric
- ½ tsp salt
- ½ tsp pepper
- ¼ cup chopped cilantro, roughly chopped
- ¼ cup chopped parsley, roughly chopped
- 2 scallions, finely chopped

1 tbsp olive oil

For the Dressing:
2 tbsp tahini
1 - 2 tbsp maple syrup
3 tbsp extra virgin olive oil
½ tsp Dijon mustard
1 tbsp freshly squeezed lemon juice
½ tsp sea salt

DIRECTIONS

Preheat the oven to 400°F / 200°C. Line a baking tray with parchment paper.

In a medium bowl add the sweet potatoes, red pepper, and chickpeas. Drizzle with 1 tablespoon of olive oil and add cumin, coriander, turmeric, salt, and pepper. Massage the oil and spices into the potatoes, pepper, and chickpeas until they are all evenly coated. Pour onto the baking tray and arrange in a single layer.

Roast for 15-20 minutes until the potato is tender when pierced with a fork.

While the vegetables and chickpeas are roasting you can prepare the rest of the salad.

Roughly chop the kale and place in a large serving bowl along with the cilantro, parsley, and scallions. Set aside.

Add all dressing ingredients to a mason jar. With the lid tightly closed shake the ingredients vigorously for a minute (or as long as you can!) until the dressing thickens and all ingredients are well combined.

Remove the vegetables and chickpeas from the oven and allow them to cool down for 15-20 minutes then add to the kale salad. Toss to combine.

Drizzle with dressing before serving.

The salad and dressing (stored separately) will keep for up to 3 days in the fridge.

QUINOA, KALE AND BLACK BEAN BURRITO

Add this filling, healthy and delicious burrito to your weight loss plan to keep you full for hours. Make a large batch to keep in the fridge for up to 3 days (except the avocado which needs to be fresh) for a quick and easy meal.

Preparation Time
30 minutes

Total Time
30 minutes

Makes
4 servings

Per Serving: Calories: 695 | Fat: 20.2g | Saturated Fat: 3.9g

INGREDIENTS

For the Kale Filling:

½ tbsp olive oil
3 cups kale, stems removed and leaves chopped
1 large garlic clove, finely chopped
1 tsp smoked paprika
¼ - ½ tsp dried chili flakes (optional depending on heat preference)
⅛ tsp salt

For the Quinoa-Bean Filling:

¾ cup quinoa, thoroughly washed
1 ½ cups vegetable stock
1 can (14oz / 400g) black beans, drained and rinsed
Handful of fresh cilantro, chopped
2 tbsp freshly squeezed lime juice

⅛ tsp black pepper

For the Pico De Gallo:

4 ripe tomatoes, finely chopped
¼ red onion, finely chopped
2 tbsp cilantro, chopped
1 tbsp lime juice
½ tsp cumin
1 jalapeno, finely chopped (optional)
Pinch of sea salt, to taste

For the Guacamole:

1 ripe avocado, pitted and peeled
½ lime, freshly squeezed
¼ ripe tomato, seeds removed and finely chopped
2 tbsp fresh cilantro, chopped
⅛ tsp salt
⅛ tsp pepper

4 large tortilla wraps

DIRECTIONS

For the Quinoa:

Bring the vegetable stock to a boil and add quinoa. Cover and cook for 10-12 minutes. Once cooked remove from heat, fluff up using a fork and stir in beans, cilantro and lime juice. Set aside.

While the quinoa is cooking heat a frying pan over medium heat then add the kale, garlic, paprika, chili, salt, and pepper. Saute for 3-4 minutes until the kale has wilted then continue to cook until any excess liquid has evaporated. Set aside.

For the Pico de Gallo:

Stir the tomatoes, red onion, cilantro, lime, cumin, jalapeno, and salt in a small bowl. Set aside.

For the Guacamole:

Mash the avocado in a small bowl and add all other ingredients, mixing well to combine. Set aside.

To Assemble the Burritos:

Working with one tortilla at a time fill the wrap with 2 heaped tablespoons of the bean mixture, 2 tablespoons of kale, 1 tablespoon of pico de gallo and 1 tablespoon of guacamole. Roll the burrito, tucking the sides in as you go along. Continue with remaining bean burritos. Slice in half before serving as it will be easier to eat this way.

You can make these ahead and keep them in an airtight container for up to 3 days, however, they are best when served fresh due to the avocado.

SPICY LENTIL & ROAST VEGETABLE WRAPS

Tender lentils and roasted vegetables make up the filling for this vibrant and tasty wrap. It's a versatile dish that allows you to use up leftover vegetables in the fridge.

Preparation Time
15 minutes

Total Time
30 minutes

Makes
4 servings

Per Serving: Calories: 500 | Protein: 19.6g | Fat: 17.4 g

INGREDIENTS

For the Lentil Filling:
2 cups of brown or green lentils, cooked

For the Roast Vegetables:

- ½ white onion, finely chopped
- ½ head broccoli, cut into small florets
- 1 red pepper, sliced
- ½ large courgette, cut into sticks
- 1 tbsp hot paprika
- 1 tsp cumin powder
- 1 tsp dried chili flakes
- ½ tsp salt
- ½ tsp pepper
- Drizzle of olive oil
- 4-6 wholewheat tortilla wraps
- 1 ripe avocado, mashed
- ¼ cup packed fresh basil leaves, roughly chopped
- ¼ cup packed fresh cilantro, roughly chopped

DIRECTIONS

Preheat the oven to 350°F/ 175°C. Line a baking tray with foil or parchment paper.

Place vegetables on the parchment paper, sprinkle with cumin, paprika, chili, and salt and drizzle with olive oil. Roast in the oven for 25 minutes until fully cooked. Remove and set aside on a plate.

Mash the avocado in a small bowl. Drain the lentils if using canned.

To Assemble the Wraps:

Working with one wrap at a time, spread ¼ of the mashed avocado in a strip in the center. Fill with a few tablespoons of the lentils and some roasted vegetables and a sprinkle of the chopped herbs. Wrap the burrito, folding in the sides as you go along. Continue with remaining wraps and slice each wrap in half when ready to serve.

Keep any leftover lentil or vegetable mixture in an airtight container in the fridge for 2 days.

STUFFED SWEET POTATO WITH QUINOA TABBOULEH

This nutrient packed meal celebrates fresh Middle Eastern flavours, is easy to prepare and makes a great meal on the go as it can also be enjoyed cold. The flavours of parsley and mint are combined with lemon, tahini and pomegranate, creating an authentic yet healthy and hearty dish.

Preparation Time 10 minutes

Total Time 55 minutes

Makes 4 servings

Per Serving: Calories: 399 | Fat: 15.7g | Saturated Fat: 2.2g

INGREDIENTS

- 4 medium sweet potatoes, scrubbed
- ½ cup / 85g uncooked quinoa, washed thoroughly
- 1 cup water or veg stock
- 1 cup fresh parsley, roughly chopped
- ⅓ cup fresh mint, roughly chopped
- ½ tbsp olive oil
- 1 small red onion, finely chopped
- 2 medium tomatoes, seeds removed and finely chopped
- Juice from ½ lemon
- ¼ tsp salt
- ½ tsp pepper
- 4 tbsp tahini
- 4 tbsp sesame seeds
- ½ pomegranate, optional

THE *Skinny* VEGAN COOKBOOK

DIRECTIONS

Preheat the oven to 350°F / 175°C. Line a baking tray with parchment paper.

Pierce a few holes in the sweet potato to allow steam to escape while they are cooking. Drizzle with a tablespoon of olive oil and use your hands to coat the potatoes as evenly as possible. Roast in the oven for 40-50 minutes. The potatoes are ready when you can easily pierce them with a fork.

While the potatoes are roasting you can make the tabbouleh salad. Heat up one cup of lightly salted water or vegetable stock. Once boiling stir in the quinoa, cover with a lid and reduce to a low simmer for 10-12 minutes. Remove from the heat without opening the lid and let the quinoa steam for 2 minutes. Uncover and fluff it up using a fork. Leave it to cool down while the potatoes are roasting.

Place the chopped parsley, mint, onion, and tomato in a large serving bowl and toss to combine. When the quinoa has cooled down add it to the mixture and pour in the lemon juice, salt, and pepper.

Remove the potatoes from the oven and slice lengthways to open them up. Add a few tablespoons of the tabbouleh, drizzle with 1 tablespoon of tahini per potato and sprinkle 1 tablespoon of sesame seeds onto each potato. Garnish with pomegranate if using.

Serve while hot.

The quinoa tabbouleh will keep for 3-4 days in an airtight container in the fridge and is great served with tahini.

CREAMY BROCCOLI & RED LENTIL DETOX SOUP

We all need a trusty detox soup recipe to help nourish us after a bad spell of eating, or for those cold winter days where our immune system needs a helping hand. This recipe combines turmeric, garlic, ginger, broccoli, lentils, and cilantro for a low calorie yet hearty and filling soup that is sure to give your body the boost it needs and keep you full for hours after.

Preparation Time
10 minutes

Total Time
20 minutes

Makes
3 servings

Per Serving: Calories: 272 | Fat: 6.8g | Saturated Fat: 0.7g

INGREDIENTS

1 tbsp olive oil
½ tsp cumin seeds
1 medium white onion, finely chopped
2 garlic cloves, minced
½ tbsp freshly grated ginger
chopped into florets
½ cup red lentils
1 cup / 250ml vegetable stock
½ tsp salt
½ tsp pepper

1 small red chili, optional
½ tsp turmeric
1 head of broccoli,
400ml unsweetened dairy-free milk
⅓ cup cilantro, chopped

DIRECTIONS

Heat oil in a large pot and once hot add the cumin seeds, stirring constantly for 30 seconds until they become fragrant and start to darken slightly.

Add the onion and saute for 3-4 minutes until soft then stir in the garlic, ginger, chili, and turmeric. Stir for a minute over low heat to ensure nothing catches on the bottom of the pan.

Add broccoli, lentils, stock, salt, and pepper. Increase the heat to medium, cover with a lid and cook for 8-10 minutes until the lentils are tender.

Stir the dairy-free milk into the mixture then using an immersion blender pulse at least ½ of the soup - or as much as you like depending on how smooth or chunky you like it. If it seems too thick add a dash more stock.

Return to the heat for 2-3 minutes then add chopped cilantro.

Serve while hot.

The soup will keep for up to 3 days in an airtight container in the fridge.

MAINS

VEGETABLE STIR-FRY WITH GINGER MISO SAUCE

Stir-fries truly are the perfect weeknight dinner - easy to make, packed full of taste and health, filling but low calorie. This richly flavoured recipe requires barely any prep, no special ingredients and provides a healthy serving of vegetables. This version is served with whole wheat noodles but you can use brown rice if you prefer.

Preparation Time
Time: 5 minutes

Total Time
15 minutes

Makes
2 servings

Per Serving: Calories: 540 | Fat: 7.5g | Saturated Fat: 1.1g

INGREDIENTS

For the Stir Fry

2 cups mixed vegetables (such as mushrooms, carrots, baby corn, green beans, edamame etc)
1 tbsp sesame oil
1 thumb-sized knob of ginger, grated
3 cloves of garlic, sliced as thin as possible
1 red chili, finely chopped

For the Ginger-Miso Sauce

3 tbsp red / brown miso paste
3 tbsp rice vinegar
2 tbsp water
2 tbsp maple syrup
2 tbsp soy sauce

5oz / 140g whole wheat noodles or rice noodles
3-4 scallions, chopped

DIRECTIONS

Cook the noodles according to packet directions.

Chop all the vegetables into equal sizes so they cook equally.

Combine the sauce ingredients in a small mug.

Heat a dry wok over medium high heat until it starts to smoke then add sesame oil, ginger, garlic, chili and the mixed vegetables. Stir fry for a minute then cover with a lid for another minute as the steam will cook the veggies faster.

Remove the lid and pour in the noodles and stir fry sauce. Fry for another minute until the vegetables are cooked but still have a bit of a bite.

Remove from the heat and top with scallions.

CARIBBEAN JERK TOFU WITH COCONUT QUINOA

This Caribbean tofu is spicy but still mellow on the pallet - exactly how a good jerk seasoning should be! The tofu is marinated in complementary yet complex flavors to create a dish that celebrates West Indian culture.

Preparation Time
Time: 20 minutes
(+ 30 minutes to marinate tofu)

Total Time
45 minutes

Makes
4 servings

Per Serving: Calories: 369 | Fat: 17.2g | Saturated Fat: 7.1g

INGREDIENTS

For the Marinade:

1.7oz / 800g extra firm tofu
1 tbsp coconut oil
1 tsp ground coriander
1 tsp dried thyme
1 tsp ground allspice
1-2 tsp chili flakes
½ tsp kosher salt
(depending on heat preference)
½ tsp ground cinnamon
1 tsp black pepper
1 garlic clove, crushed
Juice of 2 limes

For the Coconut Quinoa:

1 cup / 170g quinoa, rinsed thoroughly

1 cup / 240ml water
½ cup / 120ml unsweetened coconut milk
2 tbsp desiccated coconut
½ tsp salt

DIRECTIONS

To start, remove tofu from packaging and press between two towels to remove excess water. You can use something weighted, such as a large saucepan or a heavy chopping board and place this on top of the tofu to squeeze out as much moisture as possible for a minimum of 10 minutes. This process will allow the tofu to absorb much more flavor. After 10 minutes chop the tofu into cubes.

In a large bowl combine all marinade ingredients then stir in the tofu until each piece is evenly coated. Cover and refrigerate overnight or for a minimum of 30 minutes.

To make the quinoa bring the water, coconut milk, desiccated coconut and salt to a boil. Pour in the quinoa and give everything a quick stir, cover, reduce to a simmer and cook over low heat for 12-15 minutes. Remove from the heat, fluff the quinoa with a fork, and allow to sit, covered for a further 10 minutes.

Heat a large skillet over medium heat with a tablespoon of oil. Once the oil is hot fry the tofu in batches, turning frequently so that each side is evenly browned. Transfer to a paper towel lined plate and continue with remaining tofu cubes.

Serve tofu over coconut quinoa.

CHANA MASALA WITH SPINACH & PEAS

A quick and easy spiced chickpea and tomato dish, with the addition of spinach and peas - perfect served over freshly made basmati rice. Great tasting, super low calorie recipe with hardly any saturated fat.

Preparation Time
10 minutes

Total Time
20 minutes

Makes
4 servings

Per Serving: Calories: 226 | Fat: 5.3g | Saturated Fat: 0.7g

INGREDIENTS

1 tbsp olive oil
1 onion, finely chopped
Thumb-sized piece ginger, grated
1 large garlic clove
½ tbsp cumin seeds
2 tsp turmeric
2 tsp ground coriander
1 tsp garam masala
½ tsp dried red chili flakes (or more depending on heat preference)
4 tbsp tomato purée
2 cans (2 x 14oz /400g) can chickpeas, drained
2 cups / 500ml vegetable stock
7 oz / 200g spinach, large stalks removed, leaves finely shredded
½ cup peas, fresh or frozen
½ cup fresh cilantro, roughly chopped

DIRECTIONS

Heat the oil in a large pan and, once hot, add the cumin seeds, stirring constantly for a minute while they roast then saute the onions for 2-3 minutes. Add the garlic, ginger and all spices and stir for a minute then mix in the tomato puree.

Add the chickpeas and stock, bring to a boil, then reduce to a simmer and cook, covered, for 10 minutes.

Remove the lid and add the spinach and peas, cooking for another 10 minutes until most of the liquid evaporates.

Stir in the fresh coriander then serve over rice.

MEXICAN STYLE STUFFED PEPPERS

These Mexican peppers are packed with flavor and are a great dish for the whole family. The trick is to boil the bell peppers first as this prevents them from drying out while in the oven. You can make various substitutions depending on what you have in the pantry, making these a great versatile weeknight dinner option.

Preparation Time
15 minutes

Total Time
55 minutes

Makes
4 servings

Per Serving: Calories: 698 | Fat: 8.2g | Saturated Fat: 1.4g

INGREDIENTS

- 4 large bell peppers, any color
- 1 tbsp olive oil
- ½ medium onion, finely chopped
- 2 cloves garlic, finely chopped
- 2 cups brown rice, cooked
- 1 (14oz / 400g) can mixed beans, drained and rinsed
- ½ tsp salt
- 1 (14oz / 400g) can chopped tomatoes
- 6oz / 170g corn, tinned or frozen
- ½ tsp cayenne pepper
- 1 tsp ground cumin
- 1 tsp smoked paprika
- 1 tsp salt
- ½ tsp black pepper

DIRECTIONS

Preheat oven to 350°F / 175°C. Coat a 9x9" baking tray with a little olive oil or spray oil.

Using a small sharp knife cut the top off the peppers and scrape out the membrane and seeds. Set aside.

Heat the oil in a skillet over medium heat and fry the onion for 2-3 minutes until it has softened. Add the garlic and fry for a minute until the garlic has become fragrant. Remove from the heat.

In a large bowl combine the rice, beans, chopped tomato, corn, spices, and seasoning and mix well.

Spoon the rice mixture into each pepper, pushing it down as you go along. Continue with the remaining mixture. You may have some left over which can be kept in the fridge for 2-3 days and makes a great lunch!

Arrange the peppers in the baking dish so they are upright - you can rest them on each other for extra stability.

Cover with foil and bake in the oven for 15 minutes then remove the foil and bake for a further 5-10 minutes.

The peppers are great served with a salad.

SICILIAN EGGPLANT ROLLS WITH TOFU RICOTTA

This striking recipe uses the 'meaty' flesh of aubergines to wrap thick and creamy tofu ricotta. Silken tofu is used in replace of the more common cashew as it is much lower in calories and fat, and higher in protein. You will be surprised and how effectively the tofu replaces cheese and cashews.

Preparation Time
15 minutes

Total Time
35 minutes

Makes
4 servings

Per Serving: Calories: 269 | Fat: 13.2g | Saturated Fat: 2.3g

INGREDIENTS

For the Filling:

12oz / 340g extra firm tofu
½ lemon, juiced
½ tsp garlic powder
1 tsp Italian seasoning
2 tbsp nutritional yeast
1 tbsp olive oil
¼ tsp salt
¼ cup fresh basil leaves, finely chopped
1 cup marinara sauce

For the Aubergine:

2 large eggplants, sliced lengthwise into ¼ inch slices
1 tbsp olive oil
1 tsp dried oregano
¼ tsp salt
¼ tsp pepper

DIRECTIONS

To start, remove tofu from packaging and press between two towels to remove excess water. You can use something weighted, such as a large saucepan or chopping board and place this on top of the tofu to squeeze out as much moisture as possible for a minimum of 10 minutes.

Preheat the oven to 350°F / 175°C and prepare an 8x8" oven dish.

Combine oil, oregano, salt, and pepper in a small bowl. Brush each eggplant slice with the oil mixture. Heat a griddle pan over high heat. Once heated place 2-3 slices of eggplant (or as many as you can fit on the pan without them overlapping and reduce the heat to medium.

Fry the eggplant for 2-3 minutes on each side until they have softened and grill marks form. Continue with remaining eggplant slices and set aside.

Crumble the drained tofu using either your hands or a fork into a medium sized bowl and combine with remaining filling ingredients, except marinara sauce. Stir the mixture very well, crushing the tofu with a fork as you go along.

Evenly pour the marinara into the oven dish.

Scoop 3 tbsp of tofu ricotta into an eggplant slice and tightly roll it up. You can use a toothpick to seal the roll if you prefer. Place the roll into the oven dish, seam side down and continue with the remaining eggplant slices and ricotta.

Bake for 10-15 minutes until the sauce is bubbling and the eggplant has browned. Remove from the oven, pull out the toothpicks if using them

Serve immediately while hot.

The rolls are best on the day they were made but will keep in the fridge for 2 days.

RATATOUILLE PASTA BAKE

This quick, easy and thrifty pasta bake is the perfect way to satisfy the whole family, featuring a rich tomato base that is packed full of vegetables and bursting with Italian flavour. It's a great make ahead meal that can be prepared up to 2 days ahead and kept in the fridge until it's ready to be baked. It keeps well in the freezer in case you have leftovers or want to split it up for another easy weeknight meal.

Preparation Time
15 minutes

Total Time
1 hour 10 minutes

Makes
6 servings

Per Serving: Calories: 322 | Fat: 4.4g | Saturated Fat: 0.6g

INGREDIENTS

1 tbsp olive oil
1 medium zucchini, sliced
1 small butternut squash, chopped
2 large portobello mushrooms, sliced
2 small red onions, peeled and quartered
4 large garlic cloves, unpeeled
4 tbsp tomato puree
½ tbsp sugar
½ cup vegan red wine
2 cups / 475ml vegetable stock
1 tbsp dried Italian herb mix or herbs de Provence
1 tsp salt, divided
¾ tsp pepper
14oz / 400g dried pasta

THE Skinny VEGAN COOKBOOK

2 cans (14oz / 400g) chopped tomatoes

DIRECTIONS

Preheat the oven to 400°F / 200°C. Line a baking tray with parchment paper or foil.

Place the zucchini, butternut squash, mushrooms, onions, and garlic on the baking tray and drizzle with olive oil until evenly coated.

Roast in the oven for 20 minutes until the vegetables have softened and are starting to brown around the edges. Remove but leave the oven on and reduce the heat to 375°F / 170°C.

While the vegetables are roasting cook the pasta according to packet directions along with ½ tsp salt. Once cooked to al dente drain and pour over cold water to stop the pasta from continuing to cook. Set aside.

In a large saucepan add the chopped tomatoes, tomato puree, sugar, red wine, stock, dried herbs, ½ tsp salt, and pepper and bring the mixture to a boil. Reduce and simmer for 15-20 minutes until the sauce has thickened and reduced.

Mix in the pasta and roasted vegetables (pop the soft garlic into the sauce and discard the skin - be sure to mix the garlic into the sauce well), transfer to a baking dish, cover with foil and bake for 20 minutes. Remove the foil and bake for an extra 10 minutes.

Serve hot with a side salad.

15 MINUTE CREAMY AVOCADO-BASIL PASTA

What's not to love about this recipe! It features a smooth, creamy and luxurious avocado and basil sauce that's bursting with fresh vegetables and flavours - plus you can whip up dinner in just 15 minutes with hardly any mess!

Preparation Time
5 minutes

Total Time
15 minutes

Makes
4 servings

Per Serving: Calories: 587 | Fat: 29g | Saturated Fat: 4.5g

INGREDIENTS

13oz / 370g whole wheat pasta
2 handfuls of spinach
1 large clove garlic, crushed
Juice of half a lemon or lime
2 small ripe avocados, peeled & pitted

½ cup basil leaves
¼ tsp sea salt
¼ tsp black pepper
⅓ cup olive oil
1-3 tbsp water
Handful of cherry tomatoes or sundried tomatoes, chopped

DIRECTIONS

Bring a large pot of salted water to the boil. Cook pasta until al dente or according to packet directions. Drain and immediately place back into the pot it was cooking in. Add the spinach to the pasta and cover the pot to allow the steam to gently wilt the leaves.

While the pasta is cooking, place the crushed garlic, lemon juice, avocados, basil, salt, and pepper into a food processor and pulse until smooth and creamy, scraping the sides down as you go along. While the food processor is running pour in the olive oil in a very slow and steady stream until it has thickened. Add 2-3 tablespoons of water - only if you feel the sauce is too thick.

Pour the avocado sauce over the pasta along with the cherry or sundried tomatoes and give it a good mix. Heat up very gently for a minute until the sauce is warm.

Serve immediately.

Unfortunately, this dish does not keep too well as avocados are always best eaten fresh, however, if you do have leftovers store the pasta in an airtight container with an avocado pit sitting on top (as the pit will prevent it from browning) - but be sure to eat it the following day.

CRISPY MEDITERRANEAN TORTILLA PIZZA

Yes you can have pizza on a weight-loss diet! Ok, it's not pizza in the traditional sense but it is still delicious and satisfying. Switching from pizza dough to a tortilla wrap can cut the calories of a dish by over half. It's much faster and healthier than a traditional pizza and taste just as delicious. The tortilla, once baked, has the effect of a thin crust crispy pizza. Nutritional yeast keeps the pizza cheesy and you can still top this pizza with your favourite veggies. Voila pizza-a-la-plants!

Preparation Time	Total Time	Makes
5 minutes	15 minutes	1 serving

Per Serving: Calories: 307 | Fat: 8.8 g | Saturated Fat: 1.7g

INGREDIENTS

- 1 large wholewheat tortilla wrap
- ¼ cup marinara sauce or plain tomato sauce
- 1 heaped tbsp nutritional yeast
- 3 olives, sliced
- ¼ small red onion, thinly sliced
- 3 sundried tomatoes, sliced
- Handful of fresh basil or parsley, finely chopped

DIRECTIONS

Preheat the oven to 375°F / 175°C. Preheat a grill wire rack or pizza tray.

Lay the tortilla on a chopping board and spoon on the marinara sauce. Use the back of a spoon to smooth and ensure you have evenly coated the surface.

Sprinkle over the nutritional yeast followed by the onion, olives, and sundried tomatoes.

Carefully transfer to a wire rack or pizza tray by gently sliding it on and bake for 10-12 minutes.

Remove from the oven, top with fresh basil and leave to cool for 2-3 minutes so the crust becomes crispy. Serve immediately while fresh.

Keeps for 2-3 days, covered, in the fridge.

THE ULTIMATE QUINOA CRUST PIZZA

Finally a pizza crust recipe that requires no kneading or waiting for the dough to rise! This easy recipe simply calls for you to soak the quinoa for 6 hours or overnight in order to make the dough. Traditional dough can take a back seat as using quinoa is much healthier and lower calorie than a regular pizza crust!

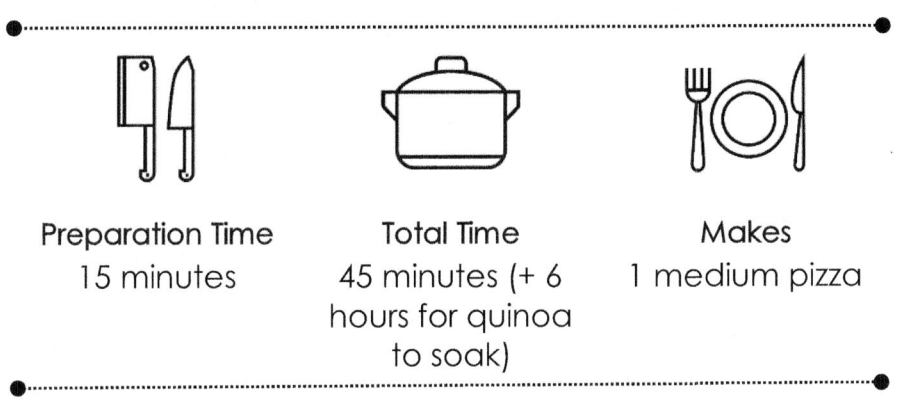

Preparation Time
15 minutes

Total Time
45 minutes (+ 6 hours for quinoa to soak)

Makes
1 medium pizza

Per Serving: Calories: 603 | Fat: 18.2g | Saturated Fat: 2.4g

INGREDIENTS

For the Crust:

¾ cup uncooked quinoa, washed thoroughly
¼ fresh water
½ tsp baking powder
¼ tsp salt
½ tbsp dried mixed herbs
½ tbsp olive oil

For the Toppings:

½ cup tomato pizza sauce
Handful of cherry tomatoes, halved
Handful of mushrooms, sliced
5-6 olives, sliced
Fresh herbs such as basil or coriander

DIRECTIONS

Place quinoa in a bowl and cover it with fresh water by at least 1 inch. Let it soak overnight or for a minimum of 6 hours.

Preheat the oven to 400°F / 200°C. Line a pizza tray or baking tray with parchment and drizzle ½ tbsp of oil over the surface. You could also use a few spritzes of spray oil.

Add the quinoa, water, baking powder, salt and herbs to a food processor and process for 4-5 minutes until you have a smooth pancake-like batter.

Evenly pour the batter onto the pizza tray and bake for 10 minutes. Remove from the oven, flip the crust over using a spatula and bake for another 10 minutes until the edges are golden brown and crisp.

If you are using mushrooms as a topping it's best to fry these in 1 tsp olive oil while the pizza is cooking. Raw mushrooms will emit too much liquid and make the crust soggy.

Remove from the oven (keeping the oven on) and spread pizza sauce over the surface to form a thin layer. Add cherry tomatoes, mushrooms and olives and place back in the oven for 5 minutes.

Garnish with herbs, slice and serve.

RED LENTIL DHAL WITH CARROT & SWEET POTATO

This quick 30-minute meal is bursting with aromatic Indian flavors with a welcoming and warming sweetness from the potatoes. You can't go wrong with this comforting, super low fat and super low calorie meal. It makes an excellent lunch too so you can always make extra for another meal during the week.

Preparation Time
10 minutes

Total Time
30 minutes

Makes
4 servings

Per Serving: Calories: 391 | Fat: 3.8g | Saturated Fat: 0.3g

INGREDIENTS

½ tbsp olive oil
1 medium red onion, finely chopped
2 garlic clove, crushed
1-inch ginger, peeled and grated
1 green chili, finely chopped
1 ½ tsp turmeric
½ tsp salt
1 ½ tsp ground cumin
2 medium sweet potatoes, unpeeled and cut into chunks
8.8oz / 250g red split lentils, washed
2 ½ cups / 600ml vegetable stock
½ tsp pepper
1 large carrot, cut into chunks
½ cup peas, fresh or frozen

1 tsp ground coriander
3 tbsp tomato puree

¼ cup fresh cilantro, roughly chopped

DIRECTIONS

Heat oil over medium heat in a large saucepan and saute the onions for 2-3 minutes. Add garlic, ginger, and chili and stir constantly for a minute before adding the turmeric, cumin, and coriander then fry for a minute more.

Add the tomato puree, sweet potatoes, lentils, stock, and seasoning and bring to a boil. Reduce to a simmer and cook, uncovered, for 10 minutes then add the carrots and cook for another 10 minutes until the liquid has reduced and the vegetables are tender.

Add the peas 5 minutes before you are about to serve.

Garnish with cilantro and serve over freshly boiled rice.

MUJADARA (LENTILS & RICE WITH CARAMELISED ONIONS)

This incredibly flavoursome dish is one you will return to time and time again. This easy to make signature dish from the Middle East consisting of rice, lentils and caramelized onions that have been infused with spices. This humble meal is the essence of comfort food. Packed with protein, fiber, and a healthy dose of vitamins from the addition of spinach and peas.

Preparation Time
15 minutes (+15 minutes to soak rice)

Total Time
45 minutes

Makes
2 servings

Per Serving: Calories: 353 | Fat: 7.8g | Saturated Fat: 1.2g

INGREDIENTS

- ½ cup long grain white rice, soaked for 10-15 minutes
- 1 large red onion, chopped
- ½ tbsp coconut or brown sugar
- 1 tsp balsamic vinegar
- 1 tbsp olive oil
- 1 tsp salt, divided
- ½ tsp sugar
- 1 tsp each: cumin powder / chili powder / paprika
- ½ tsp black pepper
- 1 cup vegetable stock
- ½ cup frozen pea

½ cup small brown lentils, washed and sorted
1 cup water

Large handful of spinach, washed

DIRECTIONS

Place the rice in a bowl, top with fresh water and leave to soak for 10-15 minutes.

Heat oil in a large pot over medium heat. Once hot add the onion and cook for 15 minutes until they start to caramelize. Reduce the heat to low and add the brown sugar, stirring while it melts then add 1 teaspoon of balsamic vinegar. Cook for a further 5 minutes.

While the onions are caramelizing, bring 1 cup of water to a boil with ½ tsp of salt and ½ tsp of sugar and add the lentils. Reduce the heat and simmer for 12 minutes until they are partially cooked. Drain and set aside.

Once the onions have finished caramelizing add cumin, chili powder, paprika, the remaining ½ tsp salt and black pepper, and stir well for a minute then mix in the stock, rice, and lentils.

Reduce to low, cover and cook for 20 minutes. Stir in peas and spinach and serve once the peas have thawed and the spinach has wilted.

CAULIFLOWER DHANSAK

A filling and hearty curry which features a medley of aromatic spices in a thick lentil gravy and tender vegetables. One serving will keep you full and satisfied for hours, preventing any snacking. The curry is slow cooked in the oven which gives the flavors time to marry and results in a wonderfully flavorsome authentic curry. Leftovers also make an excellent lunch!

Preparation Time
25 minutes

Total Time
2 hours

Makes
4 servings

Per Serving: Calories: 333 | Fat: 3.2g | Saturated Fat: 2g

INGREDIENTS

2 tsp coconut oil
2 tsp whole cumin seeds
4 whole black peppercorns
½ tbsp paprika
1 tsp coriander powder
½ tsp turmeric
¼ tsp garam masala
¼ tsp allspice
½ medium red onion, finely chopped
2 cloves garlic, crushed

1-inch piece fresh ginger peeled and grated
1 large carrot, peeled and chopped
1 small sweet potato, scrubbed and chopped
1 medium white potato, scrubbed and chopped
1 large tomato, chopped
1 (14oz / 400g) can chopped tomatoes

2 cups / 475 ml vegetable stock
7oz / 200g red split lentils
1 tbsp tamarind paste (optional)
½ tsp salt
½ tsp black pepper
½ medium cauliflower, cut into half florets
1 tbsp cilantro, freshly chopped

DIRECTIONS

Preheat the oven to 350°F / 175°C.

Heat coconut oil over medium heat in a large oven proof pot and once hot add all of the spices. Stir constantly for a minute while the spices roast and release their flavors. Add the onion and saute for 5 minutes until soft, then add the garlic and ginger.

Stir in the carrots, sweet potatotes, white potatoes, and tomato and cook for 5 minutes until the carrots start to soften.

Pour in the chopped tomatoes, stock, and lentils, salt and pepper and bring the mixture to a boil.

Transfer the dish to the oven and cook, uncovered, for 45 minutes, giving it a stir halfway through.

Mix in the cauliflower and return to the oven for 5-7 minutes. You want the cauliflower florets to have a nice 'bite' to them so don't overcook.

Remove from the oven, stir in the tamarind and coriander and serve over freshly boiled rice.

The curry will keep for 3 days, covered in the fridge, or 3 months in the freezer.

MUSHROOM & CHICKPEA PITTA BURGER

High in fiber and low in fat, these baked burgers are a healthy take on fast food that will keep you full for hours. They freeze well so are perfect for lazy dinners.

Preparation Time: 20 minutes
Total Time: 35 minutes
Makes: 4 servings

Per Serving: Calories: 486 | Fat: 11.9g | Saturated Fat: 3.1g

INGREDIENTS

- 1 tbsp olive or coconut oil
- 1 small red onion, peeled and finely chopped
- 2 large cloves garlic, crushed
- 2.6oz / 75g mushrooms (any variety you like), chopped into very small pieces
- 1 can (420g / 14.8oz) chickpeas, drained and rinsed
- 2 tbsp chickpea flour
- 1 tbsp tahini
- ½ medium apple, grated (unpeeled)
- ½ tsp ground cumin
- ½ tsp sea salt
- ½ tsp black pepper
- 2 tbsp fresh cilantro, finely chopped
- 1 medium tomato, diced
- 4 whole wheat round pitta breads
- Lettuce, tomatoes, gherkins etc, for garnishing
- 1 tbsp freshly squeezed lemon juice

DIRECTIONS

Turn on the broiler or grill setting on your oven.

Heat oil in a skillet over medium heat. Once hot saute the onions for 3-4 minutes then add the garlic and mushrooms, frying for another 5 minutes until the mushrooms have softened and started to emit some of their liquid. Remove from the heat and set aside.

In a large mixing bowl mash the chickpeas with a fork or potato masher as much as possible. It is ok to leave it a little chunky with a few whole chickpeas but the majority needs to be smooth.

Add the chickpea flour, tahini, lemon juice, grated apple, cumin, salt, pepper, cilantro, and tomato and mix together with a fork or if you prefer you can use your hands.

Add the onion-mushroom mixture and stir until combined.

Turn the grill or broiler to high heat.

Divide into 4 equal sized burgers and place on a foil-lined baking tray.

Grill for 15 minutes, turning each burger over after 8 minutes to evenly cook them on each side.

Serve inside a pitta with extra garnish such as lettuce, gherkins or tomatoes.

15 MINUTE GARLIC & MUSHROOM QUINOA

This delicious and hearty quinoa dish is full of flavor, comes together in 10 minutes and uses just 7 ingredients. All ingredients are cooked in one pot making cleanup a breeze. This is quick, easy, low calorie cooking at its finest!

Preparation Time
5 minutes

Total Time
15 minutes

Makes
2 servings

Per Serving: Calories: 420 | Fat: 12.6g | Saturated Fat: 1.6g

INGREDIENTS

1 cup quinoa, washed
2 cups water or vegetable broth
½ tbsp olive oil
10oz / 280g mushrooms (any variety), thinly sliced

5 cloves garlic, minced
1 tbsp soy sauce
½ tsp black pepper
4 tbsp fresh parsley leaves, finely chopped

DIRECTIONS

In a medium saucepan bring 2 cups of water (or vegetable broth for added flavor) to a rolling boil. Add the quinoa, cover the pot and reduce the heat to a low simmer. Cook the quinoa for 10-12 minutes. Remove from the heat and let it steam for 2 minutes without removing the lid, then use a fork to fluff it up.

THE *Skinny* VEGAN COOKBOOK

While the quinoa is cooking heat oil over medium heat, add the mushrooms and cook until they just start to soften then add the garlic, soy sauce, and black pepper. Fry for 5 minutes until some of the liquid evaporates then add the quinoa, mixing well.

Remove from the heat and stir in the fresh parsley.

Serve immediately while hot with steamed vegetables or a green salad

SIDES

SPINACH, LEMON & CHICKPEA BROWN RICE PILAF

Substituting white rice for brown provides a higher fiber content, keeping you full for longer and has fewer calories per serving. The addition of chickpeas and spinach makes this a nutritionally complete meal - and is perfect as a simple main dish or a side. This may not be as exciting as some of the other dishes, but trust us, it's filling and low calorie.

Preparation Time
10 minutes

Total Time
45 minutes

Makes
4 servings

Per Serving: Calories: 354 | Fat: 5.8g | Saturated Fat: 0.9g

INGREDIENTS

1 tbsp olive oil
2 cloves garlic, finely chopped
1 medium onion, finely chopped
1 cup long grain brown rice
1 tsp each: paprika, ground coriander, ground cumin
¼ tsp black pepper
8oz / 225g frozen spinach
15oz / 400g can chickpeas, drained and rinsed
2 cups vegetable broth
½ cup raisins (optional)
½ - 1 lemon, freshly squeezed
¼ tsp salt

¼ tsp chili powder (optional)

DIRECTIONS

In a large pot heat olive oil over medium heat then saute onions for 3-4 minutes until soft. Add garlic and fry for a minute. Add rice, paprika, coriander, cumin, chili powder, salt, and pepper and mix well, stirring constantly for a minute until the rice is fully coated.

Add the remaining ingredients, except the lemon juice and mix well, bring to a boil, cover, then immediately reduce to a low simmer.

Cook for 25 minutes without opening the lid, then remove from the heat and let the pilaf steam with the lid on for 10 minutes. Do not take the lid of until after this step.

Fluff up the rice using a fork and add the lemon juice. Add the juice of between ½ - 1 lemon, depending on how large the lemon is.

PATATAS BRAVAS WITH A CREAMY GARLIC DRIZZLE

Golden crisp potatoes served in a rich tomato sauce are commonly part of a tapas meal. This delicious side dish originated in Spain and its popularity lies in its simplicity. The potatoes in this recipe are baked instead of traditionally fried making this a really healthy meal that won't add unnecessary calories to your diet. It feels indulgent whilst being anything but...

Preparation Time
10 minutes

Total Time
20 minutes

Makes
4 servings

Per Serving: Calories: 265 | Fat: 6.3g | Saturated Fat: 1g

INGREDIENTS

For the Drizzle:

½ cup vegan mayonnaise (see recipe)
¾ tsp garlic powder
1 ½ tsp freshly squeezed lemon juice
¼ cup fresh parsley, finely chopped
Pinch of salt and pepper

For the Potatoes:

2.2lbs / 1kg new potatoes, quartered (unpeeled
1 tbsp olive oil
¾ tsp salt, divided
¼ tsp pepper
2 tsp sweet paprika (pimento

For the Bravas Sauce:

- 1 tsp olive oil
- 3 large cloves garlic, minced
- 1 can (14oz / 400g) chopped tomatoes
- 1 tsp sweet paprika (pimento)
- 1 tbsp tomato puree
- 1 tbsp red wine vinegar
- ¼ - ½ tsp crushed dried red chili flakes (depending on your heat preference)

DIRECTIONS

Preheat the oven to 375°F / 175°C. Line a large baking tray with parchment paper.

Place the potatoes and ½ tsp salt in a large saucepan and pour in cold water until they are just covered. Bring to a boil and cook uncovered for 5 minutes then remove from the heat and drain the water in a colander. Pat the potatoes dry using paper towels then transfer them to the baking tray. They must be in the single layer without overlapping otherwise they won't crisp up. You can use two baking trays if yours is not large enough to hold them all.

Drizzle with oil and sprinkle salt, pepper, and paprika until evenly coated. Roast for 40 minutes, tossing once halfway through their cooking time until they are golden brown and crispy.

While the potatoes are in the oven you can make the sauce and the drizzle. Heat the olive oil in a medium saucepan and once hot fry the garlic for a minute until fragrant. Add all other Bravas ingredients and bring to a boil. Reduce and simmer for 10 minutes until the sauce thickens and reduces. Remove from the heat.

To make the drizzle, place all ingredients in a bowl and mix thoroughly. Add 1 tbsp of water or dairy free milk if you prefer it thinner.

Serve the potatoes in a large bowl mixed with the sauce and add the drizzle on top.

TIKKA (INDIAN SPICED) CAULIFLOWER RICE

This exotic and aromatic dish is perfect served as a side to a curry and even makes a great main. The rice has a welcoming warm spice from the addition of turmeric and garam masala, and a lovely bite which works perfectly with a creamy curry. Spicy, but not too hot. A great way to lift your cauliflower rice.

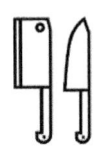

Preparation Time
5 minutes

Total Time
20 minutes

Makes
4 servings

Per Serving: Calories: 121 | Fat: 4g | Saturated Fat: 0.5g

INGREDIENT

- 1 head cauliflower (approx 1.7lbs / 800g), cut into florets
- 1 tbsp oil
- 1 tsp mustard seeds
- 1 small onion, thinly sliced
- 7oz / 200g cherry tomatoes, halved
- ½ tsp garam masala
- ¼ tsp cinnamon
- ½ tsp ground coriander
- ½ tsp turmeric
- ¼ tsp ground cumin
- ½ cup / 125ml vegetable stock
- ½ cup / 75g frozen peas
- ½ tsp salt
- ½ tsp black pepper
- 2 tbsp fresh cilantro, roughly chopped

THE Skinny VEGAN COOKBOOK

DIRECTIONS

Place the cauliflower in a food processor and pulse in short bursts until it resembles rice. Do not process for too long or you will end up with a puree! If you do not have a food processor you can use a box grater.

Heat oil over medium heat in a large frying pan and once hot add the mustard seeds, stirring constantly until they become fragrant and start popping. Add the onions and tomatoes and saute for 5-6 minutes until they have softened. Add the remaining spices and stir constantly for a minute.

Add the cauliflower and toss it around the pan to coat it with the spices then pour in the vegetable stock, peas, salt, and pepper and allow the mixture to cook for 3-5 minutes until the water has evaporated.

Garnish with cilantro and serve.

CRISPY BAKED ZUCCHINI TATER TOTS

These little tots are unbelievably delicious, just wait until you try them. A healthier and guilt free way to enjoy tater tots! These crispy bites are made with just 6 ingredients and are baked instead of fried creating a crispy outer coating but a soft and tender filling.

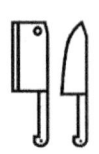

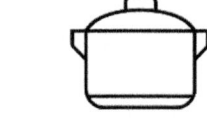

Preparation Time
15 minutes

Total Time
1 hour 10 minutes

Makes
approx 40 mini tater tots

Per 10 Tots: Calories: 237 | Fat: 3.9g | Saturated Fat: 0.6g

INGREDIENTS

- 3 large russet potatoes, washed
- 2 medium zucchinis (about 2-3 cups shredded), washed
- 1 ½ tsp salt, divided
- ¾ tsp black pepper
- 1 tsp garlic powder
- 1 tbsp olive oil

DIRECTIONS

Place the potatoes in a large pot with ½ tsp salt and cover with cold water until the potatoes are fully submerged. Bring the water to a boil and cook for around 20-25 minutes or until they are fully cooked and tender when pierced with a fork. Drain in a colander and set aside to cool down for 5 minutes until they are cool enough to touch. You need them to still be very warm - do not wait until they have cooled down to room temperature.

While you are waiting for the potatoes to cool, grate the zucchini and squeeze out as much liquid as possible using a kitchen towel or a cheesecloth. You can also use a potato ricer to squeeze out excess water. Transfer to a bowl.

Grate the potatoes and add them to the zucchinis along with the salt, pepper, and garlic powder and mix thoroughly. It is easiest to mix this with your hands but you can use a wooden spoon if you prefer.

Preheat the oven 425°F / 220°C and line a baking tray with parchment paper. You may need two baking trays depending on their size.

Use your hands to form tater tots from 1 tablespoon of the mixture and place on the prepared baking tray. Continue with the remaining mixture. Ensure you have left enough space in between each tater tot to allow them to crisp up.

Place a tablespoon of oil in a small bowl and brush each tot with a little to help them go golden brown and crisp.

Bake for 35-40 minutes or until golden brown and crispy.

FAT-FREE CRISPY POTATOES

Here's the secret recipe for the crispiest, fluffiest and most addictive potatoes - without a drop of oil! It's best to keep the skin on as this is where most of the nutrients are, plus they have more of a rustic feel but feel free to peel them if you prefer.

Preparation Time
5 minutes

Total Time
45 minutes

Makes
4 servings

Per Serving: Calories: 183 | Fat: 0.3g | Saturated Fat: 0.1g

INGREDIENTS

2.2 lbs / 1kg Yukon Gold or Russet Potatoes (scrubbed and unpeeled)
1 ½ tbsp all purpose flour
2 tsp garlic powder
1 tsp onion powder
1 tbsp paprika
½ tsp pepper
1 ½ tsp kosher salt, divided

DIRECTIONS

Preheat the oven to 420°F / 220°C. Line a baking tray with parchment paper.

Cut the potatoes into chunks of around 1" thick and place them in a large saucepan with 1 tsp salt. Pour over enough cold water to just submerge the potatoes then turn the heat to high. Once the water starts boiling set a timer for 5 minutes then remove from the heat and drain thoroughly in a sieve.

In a small bowl combine the flour, garlic powder, onion powder, paprika, ½ tsp salt and pepper.

Place potatoes back in the saucepan you used to boil them or a clean large bowl if you prefer, and evenly sprinkle the flour-seasoning mixture over the potatoes, giving them a good mix to ensure each potato cube is covered.

Transfer to the baking tray and move the chunks around so they are not overlapping and are all in a single layer.

Bake for 20-25 minutes then serve immediately while hot and crispy.

CARROT & PARSNIP FRIES

These make a great change from the regular potato fries and also allow you to ensure your diet is as varied as possible. Carrots are a great source of beta-carotene, and parsnips contain high levels of potassium. These oven baked fries make a great side dish to accompany a main meal.

Preparation Time
5 minutes

Total Time
20 minutes

Makes
3 servings

Per Serving: Calories: 198 | Fat 9.9g | Saturated Fat 1.4g

INGREDIENTS

- 3 large carrots, peeled
- 2 large parsnips, peeled
- 1 tbsp cornflour
- 2 tbsp olive oil
- 1 tsp paprika
- 1 tsp garlic powder
- ½ tsp salt
- ½ tsp pepper

DIRECTIONS

Preheat the oven to 430°F / 220°C. Line a baking tray with parchment paper.

Cut the carrots and parsnips into the shape of fries. Place in a mixing bowl and evenly coat with cornflour. Drizzle olive oil, paprika, garlic, salt, and pepper and mix well.

THE *Skinny* VEGAN COOKBOOK

Place the carrots and parsnips in a single layer on the baking tray and roast for 15-20 minutes, giving them a mix after 10 minutes to ensure they cook evenly.

Remove from the oven and place on a serving plate.

SPICY MAPLE-GARLIC ROASTED CAULIFLOWER

This cauliflower, when coated with the sticky maple sriracha, goes beautifully crisp around the edges and starts to caramelise when baked in the oven. This incredibly easy recipe is great as an entree, a side dish, or even a healthy snack when you're feeling hungry. Surprisingly low calorie for how rich and sticky it goes!

Preparation Time
10 minutes

Total Time
20 minutes

Makes
2 servings

Per Serving: Calories: 261 | Fat: 9.4g | Saturated Fat: 1.3g

INGREDIENTS

½ large head of cauliflower, cut into bite-sized florets
1 tbsp sesame oil (or olive oil)
½ tsp sea salt
1 ½ tbsp soy sauce
½ - 1 tbsp Sriracha (depending on heat preference)

4 tbsp maple syrup
¼ tsp white pepper
1 tsp garlic powder or 2 garlic cloves, minced
1 tbsp cornstarch (or arrowroot powder)
4 tbsp cold water
1 tbsp sesame seeds
2 scallions, finely chopped

THE *Skinny* VEGAN COOKBOOK

DIRECTIONS

Preheat the oven to 400°F / 200°C and line a baking tray with parchment paper.

Place the cauliflower in a single layer on the baking tray and drizzle 1 tablespoon of sesame oil over them, coating evenly. Sprinkle with sea salt and roast in the oven for 10-15 minutes, turning each floret after 7 minutes.

While the cauliflower is roasting combine maple syrup, soy sauce, sriracha, white pepper, and garlic in a small saucepan over medium heat. Bring the mixture to a simmer then reduce the heat to low, stirring frequently.

In a small bowl combine cornstarch and water until it has completely dissolved then pour into the sauce. Stir frequently for 2 minutes while the sauce thickens.

Once the cauliflower has finished roasting remove it from the oven and transfer to a large bowl. Pour the sriracha sauce over it and mix gently to coat each floret.

Return the cauliflower to the oven and roast for 2-3 minutes for the sauce to become sticky and the cauliflower to caramelise.

Top with sesame seeds and scallions. Serve immediately over freshly steamed rice or noodles.

BUTTER BEAN DIP WITH GARLIC & HERBS

A fantastic oil-free snack that's loaded with fibre and is sure to fill you up. It's super creamy and can be made in just minutes using simple ingredients you are likely to have in your kitchen. The dip is a great alternative to hummus and is perfect served with chopped veggies or toasted pitta bread wedges.

Preparation Time
10 minutes

Total Time
10 minutes

Makes
2 servings

Per Serving: Calories: 260 | Fat: 9.7g | Saturated Fat: 1.9g

INGREDIENTS

- 1 can (14oz / 400g) white beans e.g. cannellini/butter beans etc
- 1 tbsp olive oil
- 2 large garlic cloves, crushed
- 1 tsp tahini
- 4 tbsp chives, finely chopped
- 2 tbsp freshly squeezed lemon juice
- ½ tsp salt
- ¼ tsp pepper
- 3 tbsp coriander, finely chopped
- 3 tbsp parsley, finely chopped

DIRECTIONS

Drain the beans and thoroughly rinse them, then transfer to a food processor.

Heat a skillet with olive oil and fry the garlic for a minute until it becomes fragrant. Keep a close eye on it as it can burn quickly. Remove from the heat and transfer to the food processor along with the tahini, lemon juice, salt, and pepper. Process for 1-2 minutes, scraping down the sides until the dip is completely smooth. Add a tablespoon of water if the dip feels a little thick.

Add the herbs and pulse once or twice to mix them in.

Transfer the dip to a bowl and chill in the fridge for an hour. The dip is best served chilled but can be served immediately if you prefer.

The dip will keep for 3-4 days in an airtight container in the fridge.

DESSERTS & TREATS

SILKY SMOOTH CHOCOLATE PUDDING

This 6 ingredient pudding is creamy and indulgent, yet surprisingly healthy. The pudding is packed with healthy fats, calcium, magnesium, iron and is high in fibre - so you can't feel too guilty indulging in this dessert! It is high calorie so should be a special treat!

Preparation Time
5 minutes

Total Time
5 minutes (+20 mins to chill)

Makes
1 serving

Per Serving: Calories: 497 | Fat: 34g | Saturated Fat: 8.9g

INGREDIENTS

1 ripe avocado, peeled and pitted
¼ cup raw cocoa powder
1-2 tbsp maple syrup
½ tsp vanilla extract Pinch of salt

1 tbsp cacao nibs, optiona
1 tbsp fresh mint leaves or orange zest to serve (optional)

DIRECTIONS

Place all ingredients, except for the cacao nibs, in a food processor or high speed blender and pulse until completely smooth.

Transfer to a serving bowl and top with cacao nibs.

Chill for a minimum of 20 minutes before serving. The pudding is best served on the day it was made.

Top with cacao nibs and add a few mint leaves or a few strands of orange zest for some flavor variation.

CHOCOLATE QUINOA CRUNCH BARS

Made with just 6 ingredients, and no oven needed, these homemade snack bars are chocolate heaven! They are gluten free, refined sugar-free, dairy-free and best of all just 128 calories per bar.

Preparation Time
10 minutes

Total Time
20 minutes (+ 2 hours to chill)

Makes
8 bars

Per Bar: Calories: 128 | Fat: 4.2g | Saturated Fat: 0.8g

INGREDIENTS

1 cup / 25g puffed quinoa
½ cup / 75g Medjool dates, pitted
½ cup / 125g natural nut butter (peanut, almond or cashew)
¼ cup / 60ml agave nectar, brown rice syrup or maple syrup
⅛ tsp salt
2.8 oz / 80g dark vegan chocolate (70% or more)

DIRECTIONS

Place dates in a medium bowl and pour boiling water over to cover them. Leave to soak for 10 minutes then drain well and place in a food processor along with the nut butter, syrup, and salt. Process until smooth and thick, scraping down the sides as you go along to ensure the whole mixture is evenly combined.

Transfer to a large mixing bowl and fold in the puffed quinoa and chocolate chips. The mixture will be very stiff so a wooden spoon is best - or if you prefer you can use your hands.

Line a brownie tin with parchment paper and spread the mixture evenly - using the back of a spoon to smooth over the top.

Place the bars in the fridge and allow them to set for 2-4 hours before slicing and serving.

The bars will keep for 5 days in the sealed container in the fridge.

4 INGREDIENT HEALTHY FUDGY BROWNIES

Satisfy your sweet tooth with these super healthy, flourless and refined sugar-free vegan brownies which can be whipped up in just 20 minutes! These dark, rich and fudgy brownies are made with basic ingredients that you are likely to already have in your pantry - and are perfect as a quick snack on the go.

Preparation Time
10 minutes

Total Time
20 minutes

Makes
6 squares

Per Square: Calories: 217 | Fat: 12.5g | Saturated Fat: 3.3g

INGREDIENTS

1 cup / 250g sweet potato, peeled
½ cup / 125g smooth nut butter (peanut, almond or cashew butter)
⅓ cup cocoa powder

2-3 tbsp agave nectar, maple syrup or brown rice syrup (depending on how sweet you would like the brownies)
½ cup vegan chocolate chips or cacao nibs (optional)

DIRECTIONS

Preheat the oven to 350°F / 175°C and line a 6x6 brownie tin with parchment paper.

Roughly chop the sweet potatoes, place them in a medium saucepan and pour over cold water until they are just covered. Bring to a boil and cook for up to 15 minutes or until the potatoes are soft and tender when pierced with a fork. You could also steam the potatoes if you prefer.

Leave the potatoes to cool down slightly then transfer to a food processor or blender along with the remaining ingredients, except chocolate chips or cacao nibs. Pulse until the ingredients have just combined - you do not want to process it for too long. If the mixture seems a little too wet add a tablespoon of cacao powder if it seems too dry add a tablespoon of dairy free milk. Fold in chocolate chips.

Transfer the mixture to the brownie tin and smooth over the top with the back of a spoon. If the mixture sticks to the spoon you can run it under very hot water which will make it easier to create a smooth surface.

Bake for 12-15 minutes or until a toothpick comes out clean. Leave the brownie to cool in the pan for 30 minutes before removing and slicing.

The brownies will keep for 5 days in an airtight container in the fridge.

BAKED RED VELVET DOUGHNUTS

Red velvet is known for its pinkish red color and slightly chocolatey taste - and these doughnuts tick both boxes. They are baked instead of fried, reducing the calories by a considerable amount.

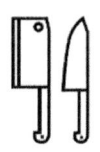

Preparation Time
10 minutes

Total Time
20 minutes

Makes
5 servings

Per Serving: Calories: 259 | Fat: 12.3g | Saturated Fat: 10.3g

INGREDIENTS

⅔ cup unsweetened dairy free milk
1 tsp apple cider vinegar
½ cup coconut sugar
¼ cup coconut oil
1 tsp vanilla extract
3 tbsp beetroot juice

1 cup all purpose flour (you can also use gluten-free flour)
½ tsp baking soda
¼ tsp baking powder
2 tbsp raw cacao powder
⅛ tsp salt

DIRECTIONS

Heat the oven to 350°F/ 175°C. Spray a doughnut pan with cooking spray.

Combine milk and vinegar in a small bowl and set aside to curdle. This will become vegan buttermilk after a few minutes.

In a medium bowl combine the sugar, coconut oil, vanilla, and beetroot juice.

In a separate bowl sieve the flour and add baking soda, baking powder, raw cacao powder, and salt and whisk together.

Pour the buttermilk into the sugar mixture and mix well, then mix the dry ingredients into the wet until just combined, making sure to not overmix. Add another tablespoon of beetroot juice if you want a more vibrant color.

Transfer the mixture to the doughnut pan, filling each mould about half way up as the doughnuts will rise in the oven. You can do this in a piping bag if you prefer a neater finish.

Bake on the center rack for 10-12 minutes until the doughnuts spring back when touched, or a toothpick comes out clean.

Allow the doughnuts to cool in the pan for 15 minutes, then gently remove them using a knife to circle around the edges.

The doughnuts will keep in the fridge for 2-3 days in a sealed container but are best eaten on the day they are made.

CHOCOLATE ORANGE CHIA PUDDING

This wonderful desert is the perfect combination of healthy eating mixed with a little indulgence. Chia seeds absorb 10x their weight in water and are a great source of slow release energy. When left in the fridge they transform basic ingredients into a rich, creamy and decadent dessert that is super healthy and low calorie.

Preparation Time
5 minutes

Total Time
4 hours or overnight

Makes
2 servings

Per Serving: Calories: 260 | Fat: 9.7g | Saturated Fat: 1.8g

INGREDIENTS

- 1 cup / 240ml unsweetened dairy free milk
- ¼ cup / 40g chia seeds
- 3 tbsp raw cacao powder, sieved
- 1 tsp vanilla extract
- 3 tbsp freshly squeezed orange juice
- 1 tsp orange zest
- 1 tbsp maple syrup, agave nectar or brown rice syrup
- 1 tbsp cacao nibs (optional)

DIRECTIONS

In a mason jar or an airtight container mix all ingredients together until well combined.

THE *Skinny* VEGAN COOKBOOK

Cover and refrigerate for a minimum of 4 hours or preferably overnight.

Serve with a freshly cut orange, coconut cream, berries or extra cacao nibs.

CARROT CAKE BITES WITH 'CREAM CHEESE' FROSTING

There's everything to love about these no-bake bite-size carrot cake treats. They're surprisingly healthy and require just 5 minutes prep time. To make these even more delicious they're topped with a thick and creamy cashew frosting that's reminiscent of traditional cream cheese frosting.

Preparation Time
5 minutes (+ 4 hours to soak cashews)

Total Time
25 minutes

Makes
16 truffles

Per Truffle: Calories: 187 | Fat: 14.3g | Saturated Fat: 4.7g

INGREDIENTS

For the Carrot Cake Bites:

- 2 cups / 100g carrot, peeled and grated
- 1 cup / 150g raw walnuts
- 1 cup / 100g Medjool dates
- 2 tbsp oats
- 1 tbsp almond meal
- 2 tbsp unsweetened desiccated coconut
- 1 tsp vanilla extract
- 1 tbsp chia seeds
- 1 tsp cinnamon
- ¼ tsp nutmeg
- ⅛ tsp salt

For the Icing:

THE *Skinny* VEGAN COOKBOOK

1 cup / 150g raw cashews (soaked for 4 hours or overnight)
3 tbsp agave syrup, maple syrup or brown rice syrup
1 tsp vanilla essence

¼ cup / 50g melted coconut oil
½ tbsp freshly squeezed lemon juice
1-2 tbsp dairy free milk

DIRECTIONS

Place all carrot cake ingredients in a food processor and process until fully combined.

Roll a tablespoon of the mixture into a ball in between the palm of your hands and place in an airtight container or a large plate (which you can cover with plastic wrap). Continue with the remaining mixture and freeze while you move onto the frosting.

Clean the food processor so that there are no remaining carrot cake ingredients. Place all cream cheese frosting ingredients into the food processor and blitz until completely smooth, scraping down the sides a few times to ensure everything is well mixed. Add 1 tablespoon at a time of dairy free milk if you prefer your frosting to be thinner.

Remove the carrot cake bites from the freezer and use a fork to dip each bite into the frosting. Continue with remaining bites then chill in the fridge for 1 hour before serving.

The carrot cake bites will last for 3-4 days in a sealed container in the fridge.

150-CALORIE CHOCOLATE COCONUT CUPCAKES

A delicious chocolate coconut cupcake for 150 calories! How could anyone resist! These are perfect for when you feel like baking a tasty treat but don't want to consume hundreds of unnecessary calories and fat. These cupcakes are versatile so you can play around with flavours. Why not try chocolate orange, vanilla and raspberry or lemon flavour...

Preparation Time
5 minutes

Total Time
30 minutes

Makes
12 cupcakes

Per Cupcake: Calories: 157 | Fat: 6.4g | Saturated Fat: 5.2g

INGREDIENTS

- ¾ cup / 180 ml unsweetened coconut milk (from a carton not a can)
- ½ tsp apple cider vinegar
- ¾ cup / 190ml agave nectar
- 2 ½ tbsp desiccated coconut
- 125g / 1¼ cup spelt flour, sieved
- 1 tsp vanilla extract
- ½ tsp bicarbonate of soda
- 1 tsp baking powder
- Pinch of salt
- ¼ cup / 30g raw cacao powder
- ⅓ cup / 50g dairy-free chocolate chips

DIRECTIONS

Preheat the oven to 350°F / 175°C. Line a muffin tin with 12 cupcake liners.

In a medium bowl mix the coconut milk, vinegar, agave, and vanilla extract.

In a separate bowl mix the flour, baking powder, baking soda, salt, and raw cacao until well combined.

Slowly pour the flour mixture into the coconut milk mixture and whisk together until you have a lump-free batter. Fold in the chocolate chips and coconut, and divide the batter equally between the muffin liners.

Bake for 20-22 minutes or until a toothpick comes out clean.

Leave to cool for 15 minutes before servings.

The cupcakes will keep for up to 4 days stored in a cake tin at room temperature.

CHOCOLATE & ALMOND ENERGY BITES

Ensuring you are getting enough protein is an important element of losing weight as it will keep you full and prevent you from getting hungry. These tasty bites are great as a pre or post workout snack, or as a treat after dinner. If you don't have time for breakfast (or just don't want to have breakfast!) these make the perfect snack.

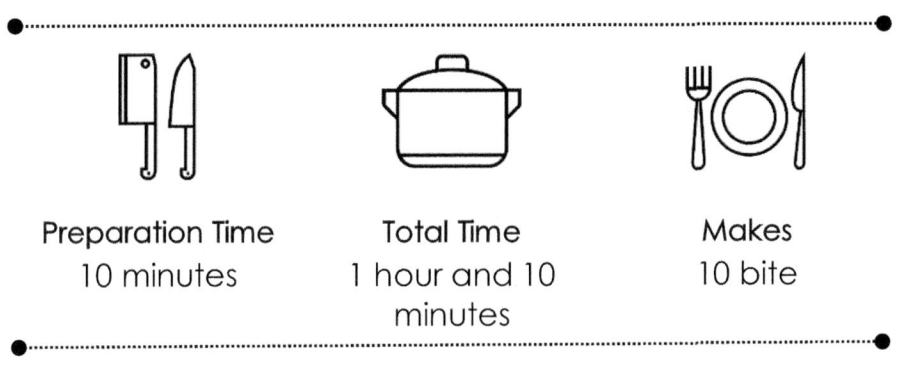

Preparation Time
10 minutes

Total Time
1 hour and 10 minutes

Makes
10 bite

Per Bite: Calories: 228 | Fat: 11g | Saturated Fat: 2.8g

INGREDIENTS

6oz / 170g raw almonds
12oz / 340g Medjool dates, pitted
3 heaped tbsp raw cacao powder
⅛ tsp sea salt
1 tbsp coconut oil, melted
2 tbsp desiccated coconut

DIRECTIONS

Place almonds in a food processor and pulse until they resemble fine breadcrumbs. Remove and transfer to a large bowl.

Place dates in the food processor (no need to wash away almond residue) and pulse until the dates have completely broken down and have become a sticky ball. Add the raw cacao, sea salt and coconut oil and pulse again until combined. Finally, pour in the almonds and pulse just a few times until well mixed.

Place the desiccated coconut on a large plate and shake it so the shreds evenly coat the entire surface.

Take a tablespoon of the mixture and roll in between the palms of your hands into small balls. You can lightly coat your palms in a little hot water if you find the mixture is sticking too much.

Place each ball on top of the coconut and gently roll it around then set aside. Repeat with remaining mixture and transfer all the balls to the freezer for an hour before serving.

The balls will keep for a week in an airtight container in the fridge.

SUPER SEED OMEGA BOOST ENERGY BARS

These simple, soft, and chewy energy bars are packed with vitamins, minerals, omega oils, and fibre - making the perfect breakfast, snack or post workout boost. Omega 3 fats are essential for various bodily functions including the brain, immune system and your heart. These bars are a great way to get your daily dose of these essential vitamins, minerals and fats.

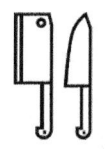

Preparation Time
20 minutes

Total Time
20 minutes (+ 4 hrs for the bars to chill)

Makes
10 bars

Per Bar: Calories: 249 | Fat: 11.6g | Saturated Fat: 1.9g

INGREDIENTS

1 ½ cups rolled oats
½ cup mixed nuts, roughly chopped and toasted if preferred
8-10 Medjool dates
2 tbsp hemp seeds
2 tbsp pumpkin seeds
2 tbsp ground flax seeds
½ tsp cinnamon
2 tbsp chia seeds
1 tbsp sesame seeds
¼ cup maple syrup, brown rice syrup or agave nectar
¼ cup natural nut butter (peanut, almond or cashew)
¼ tsp salt

DIRECTIONS

Unless your dates feel soft, plump and moist soak them in warm water for 5-10 minutes. Drain, blot dry with a kitchen towel and remove the pit.

Place dates in a food processor and pulse until they become a sticky ball of dough. Transfer to a large mixing bowl and add the hemp, pumpkin, flax, chia, and sesame seeds, mixing well. It may be easier to mix this using your hands or use a wooden spoon if you prefer.

Warm maple syrup and nut butter in a small saucepan over low heat until it has melted then remove from the heat and add the cinnamon and salt. Pour this mixture over the oats and seeds. You can either wait for the mixture to cool down and use your hands again, if not a wooden spoon is best.

Line an 8x8 brownie tin with parchment paper and transfer the mixture into the tin. Using the back of a spoon dipped in boiling hot water smooth the mixture into an even layer.

Place a sheet of plastic wrap over the bars and use something weighted such as a glass to press down firmly in order to compress the mixture. This will help them form solid bars when they have cooled.

Leave the plastic wrap covering the bars and chill in the fridge for a minimum of 4 hours before slicing into 10 bars.

The bars will keep in plastic wrap or in an airtight container for up to 10 days.

EXTRAS

CHOCOLATE HAZELNUT MILK (NUTELLA MILK)

This completely raw & natural milk is sweetened with dates and uses raw cacao powder instead of processed cocoa, providing a healthy serving of fiber, antioxidants, and vitamin E. This chocolate milk is so sweet and creamy, you'd never know it was refined sugar-free, gluten free, and vegan! It is not entirely low calorie due to the nuts, however it is healthy and a great way to kill a sweet tooth craving.

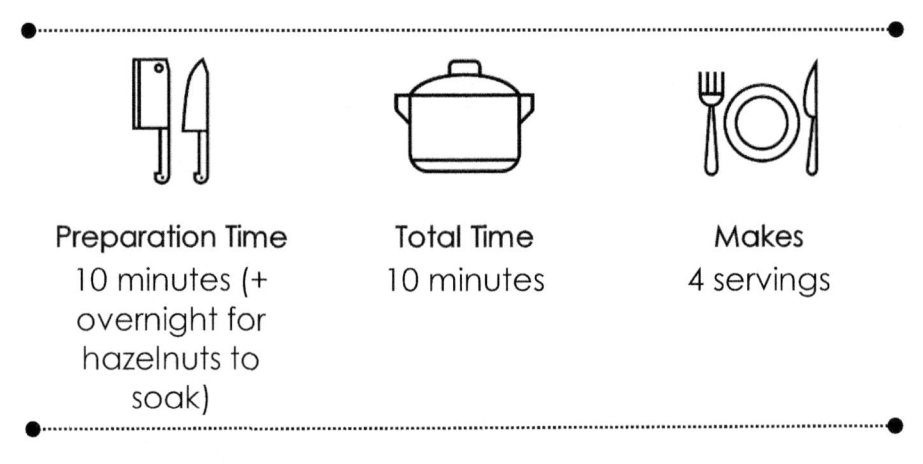

Preparation Time
10 minutes (+ overnight for hazelnuts to soak)

Total Time
10 minutes

Makes
4 servings

Per Serving: Calories: 243 | Fat: 11.8g | Saturated Fat: 1.1g

INGREDIENTS

1 cup raw hazelnuts*, soaked overnight
4 cups filtered water
2 ½ tbsp raw cacao powder
2 tsp vanilla extract

5 Medjool dates, pitted and soaked for 10 minutes in boiling water
¼ tsp cinnamon (optional)

*You can choose whether you wish to leave the skin of the hazelnuts on or off. Leaving them on makes the milk more nutritious but removing them yields a smooth milk

DIRECTIONS

Drain and rinse the hazelnuts, discarding the soaking water. Place them in a blender with the water and blend for 2-3 minutes until the nuts have completely broken down.

Pour the mixture into a nut bag or cheesecloth that has been placed over a suitably sized bowl and squeeze out as much liquid as possible from the bag.

You can save the hazelnut pulp and freeze it for use at a later date in numerous recipes.

Rinse out the blender and pour the mixture back in, along with the raw cacao, vanilla, dates, and cinnamon if using.

Blend for 2-3 minutes until completely smooth. You can strain the mixture through the cheesecloth or nut bag again if you would like a super smooth nut milk.

Serve immediately or store in the fridge in a sealable jar or bottle for 3-4 days.

EASY HOMEMADE TORTILLAS

Only four basic ingredients are needed for this foolproof and absolutely delicious tortilla recipe. These healthy whole-wheat wraps are soft and tender, with just a little bit of a 'chew'. They are perfect as a snack, for a lunch wrap or to make healthy oven baked tortilla chips.

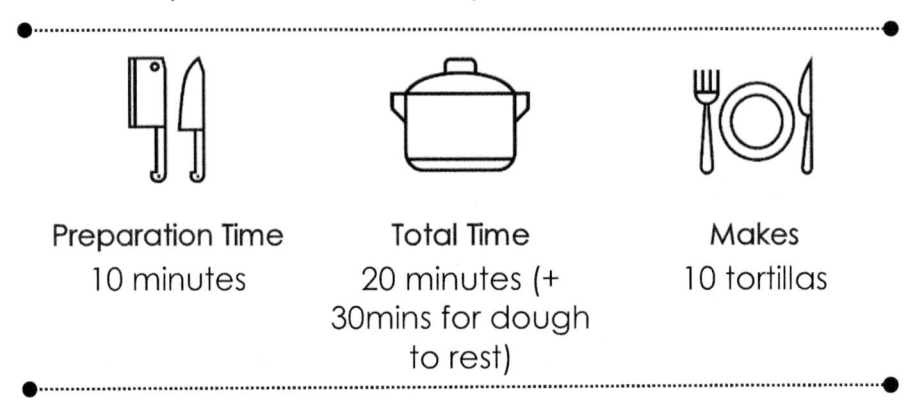

Preparation Time
10 minutes

Total Time
20 minutes (+ 30mins for dough to rest)

Makes
10 tortillas

Per Tortilla: Calories: 101 | Fat: 1.6g | Saturated Fat: 0.2g

INGREDIENTS

2 cups whole wheat flour
½ tsp salt

⅔ cup warm water
Drizzle of Oil, for frying

DIRECTIONS

In a large bowl combine flour and salt. Add the olive oil and mix in until well combined.

Add the warm water, a few tablespoons at a time while stirring until a rough dough is formed.

Transfer the dough to a lightly floured work surface and knead for 5 minutes. Return the dough to the bowl, cover and let it rest for 20-30 minutes.

Divide the dough into 8 equal sized pieces and roll each piece into a ball, pressing it down gently with the palm of your hand to flatten it. Do this on a lightly floured surface to prevent the dough from sticking.

Roll each ball into a thin circle, replicating the thickness of a tortilla.

Heat a large skillet over medium-high heat with a small drizzle of oil. Fry the tortilla on one side until bubbles start to form, between 30 seconds - 1 minute, then flip it over for another 30 seconds. The tortilla is ready when it starts to puff up.

Remove and transfer to a plate, then cover with a kitchen towel as the steam will keep them soft.

Continue with remaining dough.

Serve immediately while warm. The tortillas will keep in the fridge, covered in plastic wrap for 2-3 days or can be frozen for up to 3 months. Thaw well and reheat in the microwave for 20-30 seconds before serving.

ROASTED CHICKPEAS 3 WAYS

Chickpeas transform from a staple pantry item into a crispy, crunchy golden brown snack that you can eat, guilt free, making them the perfect healthy low-calorie snack. They are great to travel with and stay crisp for a few days. You can play around with flavors too so you will never get bored!

Preparation Time
10 minutes

Total Time
20 minutes

Makes
4 servings

Per Serving: Calories: 123 | Fat: 3.7g | Saturated Fat: 0.5g

INGREDIENTS

1 can (14oz / 400g) chickpeas, drained and rinsed

Salt and Vinegar:

1 ½ cups white vinegar
2 tsp olive or coconut oil
½ tsp sea salt

Soy & Sesame:

2 tbsp soy sauce
2 tsp sesame oil
½ tbsp sesame seeds

Chili & Lime:

Juice from 1 lime
1 tsp crushed red chili flakes
½ tsp ground cumin

½ tsp sea salt

THE Skinny VEGAN COOKBOOK

DIRECTIONS

Preheat the oven to 400°F / 200°C. The chickpeas need 25-30 minutes in the oven, giving them a good shake to evenly roast then after 15 minutes of roasting. Keep an eye on them during the last 10 minutes of cooking as they are prone to burning. Leave them to cool for 10 minutes after they have finished roasting as this is the time they will become crispy.

For Salt & Vinegar Chickpeas:

Place chickpeas and vinegar in a medium saucepan and bring the liquid to a boil (you need enough vinegar to fully submerge the chickpeas so use more or less than 1 ½ cups). Make sure you open as many windows as possible and use your air vent as the smell from the vinegar will be strong!

Once the vinegar starts to boil remove the saucepan from the heat and allow the chickpeas to sit in the vinegar for 20 minutes. Sprinkle with salt and roast.

For Soy & Sesame:

Mix the chickpeas, soy sauce, and sesame oil in a large bowl then transfer to a baking tray. Once roasted sprinkle with sesame seeds before leaving them to cool down.

For Chili & Lime:

Mix the chickpeas, lime juice, chili, and cumin together in a mixing bowl. Leave to marinade for a minimum of 10 minutes, or overnight if possible. Sprinkle with salt just before roasting.

CUMIN & CAYENNE SUPER SEED CRACKERS

These fiber rich and omega packed crackers are perfect for a quick afternoon snack, a healthy lunch or to pop in your bag if you are on the go. They will keep for a week and are great with hummus, white bean dip or even mashed avocado. You can play around with flavors too, such as rosemary & thyme, garlic & onion or even cheese with the addition of nutritional yeast.

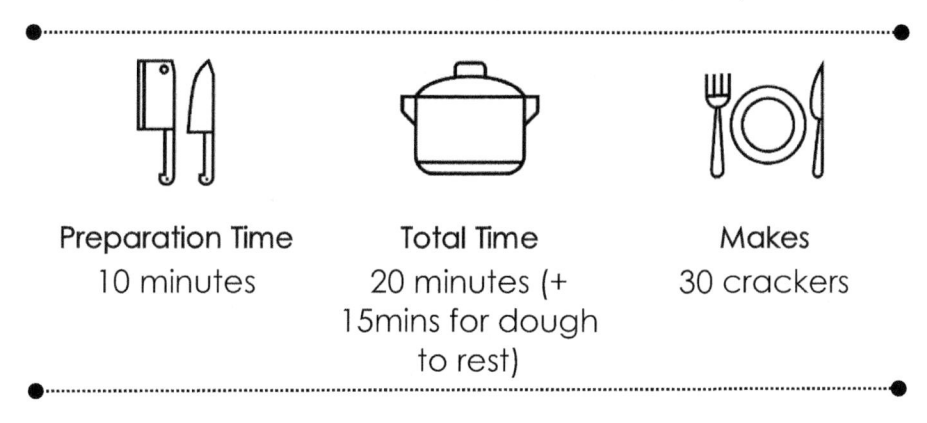

Preparation Time
10 minutes

Total Time
20 minutes (+ 15mins for dough to rest)

Makes
30 crackers

Per 3 crackers: Calories: 128 | Fat: 10g | Saturated Fat: 1.3g

INGREDIENTS

- ¼ cup whole flaxseeds
- ¼ cup chia seeds
- ½ cup sunflower seeds
- ½ cup pumpkin seeds
- ½ cup poppy seeds
- ½ tsp salt
- ½ tsp garlic powder
- ½ tsp cayenne (or more if you prefer it spicier)
- ½ tsp cumin powder
- 1 cup water

DIRECTIONS

Preheat the oven to 350°F / 175°C. Line a baking tray with parchment paper (you may need two baking trays depending on the size of your oven).

Place all ingredients in a bowl and mix well. Leave for 15 minutes in order for the chia seeds and flaxseeds to act as a binding agent. The mixture should be very thick after 15 minutes. If it seems a little watery give it a quick stir and leave for another 10 minutes.

Evenly pour the mixture onto the parchment (the mixture needs to be spread out very thin so do this in stages to assess whether you need two baking trays) and use the back of a spoon or a spatula to spread the mixture out evenly and as thin as possible. This may take a few minutes as the mixture will be very thick.

Bake for 30 minutes, remove and cut the crackers into slices, then return to the oven for another 30 minutes. Remove and transfer to a wire cooling rack before serving.

Store the crackers in an airtight container or wrapped in a paper bag at room temperature for up to a week.

HEALTHY OIL FREE HUMMUS

Finally, a hummus recipe that doesn't contain tons of oil, adding unnecessary fat and calories. This smooth and creamy hummus is almost fat-free and can be used as a filling for wraps or sandwiches, added to a buddha bowl or eaten as a super healthy snack with chopped vegetables. You may think it will lose its creaminess, but we have made this one A LOT and it's amazing and guilt-free!

Preparation Time
5 minutes

Total Time
10 minutes

Makes
4 servings

Per Serving: Calories: 91 | Fat: 2.5g | Saturated Fat: 1.7g

INGREDIENTS

1 can (15oz / 425g) chickpeas, drained and rinsed
2 cloves garlic, finely chopped
¼ - ½ tsp dijon mustard
¼ tsp ground cumin
½ tsp salt

¼ tsp pepper
2 tbsp tahini
2 tbsp almond milk
3-4 tbsp freshly squeezed lemon juice
¼ tsp paprika

DIRECTIONS

Add the chickpeas, garlic, mustard, cumin, salt, and pepper to a food processor and pulse until the chickpeas have broken down.

Add the tahini, almond milk, and lemon and continue to pulse until the hummus is completely smooth and creamy, scraping down the sides a few times as you go along. You may wish to add another tablespoon of milk if the hummus seems too thick.

Remove from the food processor and transfer to a serving bowl.

Sprinkle with paprika before serving.

10-MINUTE FAT-FREE GRAVY

A rich and delicious gravy that makes the perfect accompaniment to a nut roast, a pie or even poured on some steamed vegetables. It's ready in just 10 minutes, and produces a silky smooth, thick and rich gravy that you want to pour over everything! This one is a gamechanger if you like your gravy. All the indulgence with a fraction of the calories.

Preparation Time
5 minutes

Total Time
10 minutes

Makes
5 servings

Per Serving: Calories: 19 | Fat: 0.3g | Saturated Fat: 0.1g

INGREDIENTS

1 tbsp whole wheat or all purpose flour
1 ½ tsp vegetable stock or 1 vegetable stock cube
1 tbsp nutritional yeast (optional)
1 tsp onion powder
½ tsp garlic powder
1 tbsp soy sauce
¼ tsp black pepper
¼ tsp thyme
1-2 tsp sherry, port, Madeira (optional)
1 cup water

DIRECTIONS

Place all ingredients in a high-speed blender and pulse until completely smooth.

Pour into a saucepan and bring to a boil. Reduce to a low simmer for 5-7 minutes, stirring frequently until it starts to thicken. The gravy may not need the full 7 minutes, it is ready when it reaches the thickness you prefer.

This gravy is very adaptable. You can fry some onions or mushrooms before adding the liquid mixture.

The gravy can be made ahead by up to 3 days and reheated in a saucepan over a low heat.

HEALTHY OIL-FREE MAYONNAISE

This easy vegan mayonnaise is thick and creamy, and most importantly saves you hundreds of calories without the addition of oil. The base of this recipe is tofu so believe it or not this mayonnaise recipe is actually healthy and a great source of protein! It's perfect for sandwiches, wraps, salads or as a dip. Most importantly it doesn't compromise on taste or texture

Preparation Time
10 minutes

Total Time
30 minutes

Makes
8 servings

Per Serving: Calories: 34 | Fat: 1.8g | Saturated Fat: 0.35g

INGREDIENTS

12oz / 340g silken tofu
¼ cup dairy free milk
1 tsp apple cider vinegar
½ lemon, juiced
½ tsp Dijon mustard
½ tsp black salt (kala namak) or substitute with regular salt

DIRECTIONS

Place all ingredients in a food processor or blender and pulse until completely smooth, around 1-2 minutes. Scrape down the sides regularly to ensure all ingredients are combined. If you prefer your mayonnaise a little thinner add a tablespoon of milk at a time until you have achieved the desired consistency.

Store in an airtight container in the fridge for up to a week.

SOUR CREAM & CHIVE POPCORN

Popcorn makes a great snack for anyone looking to reduce their calorie intake as it is filling, high in fibre and low in calories. The addition of nutritional yeast adds your daily recommended amount of B12 and is also the secret ingredient for creating a wonderfully cheesy and tangy sour cream flavour. Experiment with quantities and spices to make it your own!

Preparation Time
5 minutes

Total Time
10 minutes

Makes
4 servings

Per Serving: Calories: 139 | Fat: 4.9g | Saturated Fat: 1.6g

INGREDIENTS

⅓ cup popcorn kernels
1 tbsp oil (coconut, vegetable, canola, rapeseeds etc)
3 tbsp nutritional yeast, ground into a fine powder

1 tsp onion powder
¼ tsp garlic powder
1 tsp dried chives
¼ tsp salt

DIRECTIONS

Combine nutritional yeast, onion powder, garlic powder, chives, and salt in a small bowl. Set aside.

Heat oil in a saucepan over medium heat and tilt the pan to coat the surface with the oil. Add 2-3 kernels to the pot and place the lid on. This stage allows you to test when the oil is precisely hot enough for the corn to pop so you will know when to add the remainder.

Once the kernels pop, remove the pan from the heat. Add the remaining corn then cover with the lid and give the saucepan a shake to coat them all in oil. Return the pan to the heat until the pops are more than one second apart.

Pour the spice mixture into the saucepan and use a wooden spoon to evenly coat all kernels.

Serve immediately.

THANKS FOR READING

Hope you enjoyed this book. For more great titles from High Cedar Press, check out our Amazon page and leave us a review if you have a spare minute!

Printed in Great Britain
by Amazon